There Is NO HIV

Exposing The Truth About HIV Antibody Testing
and The Metaphysics of Self-Healing through
Chakra and Kundalini Awareness

There Is N

The Rainbow Warrior

Damian Q. Laster aka Kbr AmnRkhty

THERE IS NO HIV
THE RAINBOW WARRIOR
EXPOSING THE TRUTH ABOUT HIV ANTIBODY
TESTING AND THE METAPHYSICS OF SELF-HEALING
THROUGH CHAKRA AND KUNDALINI AWARENESS

iUniverse books may be ordered through booksellers or by contacting:

iUniverse
1663 Liberty Drive
Bloomington, IN 47403
www.iuniverse.com
1-800-Authors (1-800-288-4677)

ISBN: 978-1-4917-5459-7 (sc)
ISBN: 978-1-4917-5458-0 (e)

Library of Congress Control Number: 2014921877

Printed in the United States of America.

iUniverse rev. date: 01/20/2015

PRAISE FOR DAMIAN LASTER AND RAINBOW WARRIOR

"In an age of darkness there are very few who want to see the light, let alone bring the light to others. Damian Laster is one of those people. Damian has a deep instinctive understanding of the relationship between spiritual health and physical health and his mission is sharing his insights with a planet drowning in an ocean of suffering."

~ Nancy Banks, MD, MBA, Author, *"AIDS, Opium, Diamonds and Empire, the Deadly Virus of International Greed"*

"Kudos to Damian Laster—His tireless efforts as a mostly Pro Bono Alternative Health Care Consultant have benefitted the lives of countless Americans."

~ Clark Baker, Principal Investigator, Office of Medical and Scientific Justice (OMSJ)

"Damian Laster has contributed greatly to the debate over HIV and AIDS with great humor, passion and verve."

~ David Crowe, President, Rethinking AIDS

"Damian has not only become a friend I admire and respect, he has also become a spiritual and health guide whose vast knowledge has become a template I rely greatly on, to spread information to my countrymen, who have been kept in the dark about the origins of diseases for too long...especially the pandemic that is not only crippling my country (currently holding the world record of HIV/AIDS infections) but the entire Afrikan continent. A world with people like Damian is a place humanity should celebrate."

~ Dipuo Mahlatsi, Health Activist, South Afrika.

"We are on the verge of disaster and we need Warriors to help us make it through the rain. I feel Damian Laster is one of those Warriors with the ability to guide us across difficult times. Wised up by experience, strengthened with knowledge, I believe he now knows which direction is best and I trust his guidance. I wish to every reader, the same experience of Light, Discipline and Love in which this book has been created. Thank you brother."

~ Eduardo Blanco, London, UK

"Gratitude, pride, respect, and loving solidarity are adjectives which only begin to skim the surface of the profound appreciation I have for the commitment of the soul, heart, and con- viction of Dr. Damian Laster (For many of us) To be duly engaged (only) in the mass media perspectives, opinions and dialogue(s) regarding HIV, is not only normal, but expected. Thanks to you brother/friend for inspiring this brain toward Truth, greater knowledge (of self and others), as well as expanding perspectives (especially regarding the big "business" of pain management)."

~ Dhameer D. Williams, Bermuda

"Damian Laster is a spiritual teacher and "Rainbow Warrior"- one who reveals the universal truth, helps his fellow man and spreads love throughout the world. He is also a gifted guide, storyteller and my friend. He has inspired me and many others to look deep inside to find higher energies to reach our fullest potential. As part of my growth I have needed to find self-healing. The beauty Damian emits from the heart and inner chakras has helped me on my life journey. I have found peace amidst the corruption, lies and deception of HIV/AIDS and the many other pharma and governmental traps. No mind control and/or instruments of deception can imprison us. I have learned that oppression and the criminalization of HIV cannot rule us or control our lives. Damian shows me and others a path to rise above it all and claim our position in the universe as truly free, healthy and loving beings that we were meant to be."

~ David Tavares, Toronto, Canada

Table of Contents

Acknowledgements

I thank Mother Goddess Kundalini for birthing and loving me and awakening me to my spiritual self, to wisdom and to intuition. Thank you to the Pantheon of Ancient African/Kemetan God/Goddesses, most especial Sekhmet, Heru, Anubis and Tehuti for whom I have much RAspect. Thank you Gaia, my planetary mother, for providing my earth home and for nurturing, sheltering and sustaining us earth inhabitants with food, water and shelter. I love you, too MaMa for supporting me through all life's challenges when it appeared that no one else cared. To my family and friends, I say thank you for being mirrors to my soul. A deep sense of gratitude is what I feel for nature spirits including elves, elementals, gnomes, sylphs, salamanders, undines, faeries and others that protect earth inhabitants from toxins. Thank you to all the master teachers who educate us about our spiritual selves. Great love is felt for the cosmic hierarchy, ascended masters, Galactic Federation, Guardian Alliance and benevolent extraterrestrials that guard and guide consciousness development and expansion. To internet sites that have provided a gathering place for spiritual initiates and adepts to learn and share spiritual insights and information, including but not limited to www.starseeds.net, www.isiswisdom.com, www.energeticsynthesis.com, www.resistance2010.com, www.extraterrestrials.ning.com, www.spirithousehealing.com, www.livinginblack.com www.lightgrid.com, www.Facebook.com, www.rethinkingaids.com, www.omsj.

org, and a group I created, Rainbow Warriors *The Truth About HIV* Group, on Facebook https://www.facebook.com/groups/RainbowWarriorTruthAboutHIV/. I say thank you to all the authors, writers and artists who inspired me with their words and creations. Know that you too are appreciated and loved. I offer special thanks to all those who helped make this endeavor a reality. Mrs. Gladys R. Laster, a living goddess and my amazing mother, my foremost encourager who is first and foremost in my heart, my mind and in my life. Thank you, mother. Thank you to Heru Angelo Bey and Shirley "Yanna" Brown, true friends, whose actions demonstrated their love and who encouraged me to follow my heart and my dreams. A special thanks for the organizational assistance of Lee Diogeneia. I thank graphic design artist, Di Noir Six Seth, CEO of Noir Studios. I thank iUniverse for publishing my book. Thank you readers for engaging my vision and for relating to my passions. I also want to give thanks to my ankh-estors and spirit guides. I am grateful to the master teachers who came forth to expose the HIV debacle and crisis. Their works supported and confirmed my ideas that I had been expressing and writing about since my spiritual awakening in 1998: Dr., Nancy Turner-Banks, M.D., Dr. Jewell Pookrum, M.D., Dr. Phil Valentine, Dr. Scott Whittaker, ND, Dr. Llaila Afrika, and Keidi Awadu, who is the world's leading interviewers of HIV Dissenters.

I thank and encourage all the HIV dissenters and social justice advocates all around the world who know me and my work and who also work to raise awareness of the truth about HIV. We number in the 1000s. Young Rainbow Warriors Ta'Von Powell and Isiah Powell, I appreciate your encouraging me to stand my ground. I do what I do for you. I am happy to say that each and every day I am contacted by people from all over the world who thank me for all that I do each day. I am dedicated to this mission until my last breath.

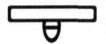

Damian Q. Laster
Conscious Doctor/Rainbow Warrior

Dedication

I dedicate this book to *Divine Mother Goddess Kundalini* and to my own divine mother, Mrs. Gladys R. Laster.

I honor the loving memory of my dear friends Everett Rachel, Ralph Manor and Jeffrey Crenshaw and Bradford Connell, gone too soon. I love you.

I also dedicate this book to you, my reader, and to every person whose eyes have met mine. Truth is available to those who have the courage to question what they have been taught. Yes, many do not want their illusions to be destroyed, but truth has no agenda. You have the innate ability to use critical thinking skills to learn to let go of what you thought was real, so that you can heal.

Introduction

"All truth goes through three stages: first, it is ridiculed; next, it is violently attacked; finally, it is held to be self-evident."

Author Unknown

T here is no HIV!

What if I told you that everything you have been told about HIV is a lie? What if I told you that for the last 30 years you have allowed yourself to be hoodwinked, duped? Would you believe me if I told you that the lesson to be learned is that the monsters in your closet and under your bed live inside of you? What if I told you that you are the only boogeyman in your life? Would you recoil in terror and denial, or would you face your demons and beat them into submission?

I am the living proof of what I teach. What I teach is that there is no HIV that is sexually transmissible and deadly. I freed myself from HIV drugs in 1998 when I realized the truth about HIV and HIV antibody testing. Yes, I am disgusted and outraged by having been lied to about HIV. Why would I not be? Hopefully, after you read my book, you will be too. More importantly, I am willing to expose the truth about this whole horrible farce using my own life as a demonstration of resilience, research, critical thinking and analysis, intuition, and wisdom gained having lived through this horrible experience and attempt on my life. I am the living proof that there is no HIV.

In this era and Age of Information, Age of Technology, Age of Enlightenment and Age of Planetary Transformation, *Mother Goddess Kundalini* led me to the truth about the alleged human immunodeficiency virus/ acquired immune deficiency syndrome (HIV); namely that receiving an HIV positive (HIV+) diagnosis means nothing of any relevance to health when understood in its proper context. There is nothing to fear from receiving an HIV+ diagnosis, because there is no HIV. There is only an HIV antibody test result, but no actual HIV virus.

Sound sinister? It is. Open your mind and your heart and journey with me.

It was as if I had been led by an invisible being or force throughout the mazes of books in libraries and bookstores as well as information on websites and articles and videos in the internet kingdom. Many authors came forward several years after my revelations in 1998 when I completed my first manuscript on this subject. Nevertheless, we came to the same conclusion: that HIV is a farce. Some of the positions of those authors will be presented in this book.

I learned that the alleged existence of HIV was a mistake from the very beginning. The so-called scientists who discovered HIV, pharmaceutical companies, big media and shady doctors are at the root of this tragedy. Alleged causes of HIV endorsed by corporate doctors have killed masses of people, millions. In many instances, faulty or misinterpreted scientific studies regarding viruses, bacteria, vaccines, pharmaceutical drug issuance and the like have paved the way for death and destruction of human life. The propagation of fear, created disease, created illness, fueled segments of the world economy, provided a means for reducing world populations, and ultimately stunted the evolution of human consciousness.

I learned that physical symptoms of bodily illnesses typically referred to as being HIV+ resulted from prolonged patterns of ill-thinking, fear and doubt, worry, shame, guilt, anger and perhaps other negative states of mind I held about myself and my condition in life. Those symptoms were not related in any way to the presence of an alleged HIV virus which was never scientifically isolated and proved to exist.

I have identified six primary myths about HIV/AIDS perpetuated by the AIDS Establishment.

1. That HIV is the same as AIDS; AIDS is caused by the HIV virus.
2. That the human immunodeficiency virus was isolated and identified using classical virology methods.
3. That HIV is sexually transmitted.
4. That AIDS is contagious.
5. That a positive HIV antibody test means death by AIDS.
6. That AIDS has no cure.

However, consider the following facts from virologists, doctors, nutritionists and researchers:
1. "Up to today, there is actually no single scientifically really convincing evidence for the existence of HIV. Not even one such retrovirus has been isolated and purified by the methods of classical virology." --Dr. Heinz Ludwig Sanger, Emeritus Professor of Molecular Biology and Virology, Max-Plank-Institute for Biochemistry, Munchen. http://www.virusmyth.com/aids/.

2. HIV has never been isolated and analyzed by standard virology protocols. Dr. Nancy Turner-Banks M.D., Aids, Opium, Diamonds and Empire: The Deadly Virus of International Greed, 2010, p. 300.

3. "AIDS is simply a new name for 25 diseases that have always existed whose causes have been listed in medical texts (Merck Manual) for over 70 years. They are: malnutrition (starvation), drugs, radiation, and chemotherapy." --Whitaker and Fleming, *Medisin*, 2010, p. 205.

4. "Nothing about HIV/AIDS has been rational." Dr. Nancy Turner-Banks M.D., Aids, Opium, Diamonds and Empire: The Deadly Virus of International Greed, 2010, p. 23.

5. "AIDS is not contagious. Nor is AIDS sexually transmitted." --Dr. Llaila Afrika, "Nutricide," 2000.

6. "...if you cannot catch healthy, then you cannot "catch sick" or AIDS[...]...An AIDS virus particle is a particle of a dead human cell. It cannot eat, reproduce, grow, move, attack you or be attacked... [...] A virus is neither retrogressive (retro=within) or progressive. A virus is dead cellular particles...[...] Most illness is the way the body's intelligence cleanses itself from poor nutrition, and toxic conditions and toxic environmental influences." --Dr. Llaila Afrika, "Nutricide," 2000, p. 105.

7. "AZT [azidothymidine], a drug so toxic that it was discarded by the Nixon administration as a treatment for cancer, and which causes AIDS, is being given to individuals because they tested positive for antibodies to an innocent virus. Though they are likely healthy at the time of administration, they will likely die from an acquired deficiency caused by AZT and

fear-induced related illnesses." --Dr. Nancy Turner-Banks M.D., Aids, Opium, Diamonds and Empire: The Deadly Virus of International Greed, 2010.

8. "The gay population became an identifiable group when they began to suffer the effects of years of drug abuse." --Dr. Nancy Turner-Banks M.D., Aids, Opium, Diamonds and Empire: The Deadly Virus of International Greed, 2010.

9. "AIDS is not a disease at all. It is a government program." --Dr. Llaila Afrika, "Nutricide," 2000.

10. "AIDS was created as a modern day fear tactic to continue the control and domination over people via sex and fear, a powerful combination, and it has worked like a charm." --Djhuty Maat Ra, 2007.

11. Typical Disclaimers from HIV Test Manufacturers

"EIA testing cannot be used to diagnose AIDS, even if the recommended investigation of reactive specimens suggest a high probability that the antibody to HIV-is present. [...] **At present there is no recognized standard for establishing the presence and absence of HIV-1 antibody in human blood. [...]** "**The Amplicor HIV-1 Monitor test is not intended to be used as a screening test for HIV or as a diagnostic test to confirm the presence of HIV infection.**"--Dr. Nancy Turner-Banks M.D., Aids, Opium, Diamonds and Empire: The Deadly Virus of International Greed, 2010, p.300.

12. "The medical consequences arising from these psychological stressors have a rational, logical, scientific explanation that has nothing to do with a phantom virus and everything to do with

what is known as deep politics."-- Dr. Nancy Turner-Banks M.D., Aids, Opium, Diamonds and Empire: The Deadly Virus of International Greed, 2010, p.13.

Scientists still are unable to tell us exactly what so-called HIV is and/or AIDS, except to say that AIDS is generally represented by a variety of illnesses brought on by opportunistic infections that invade the body yielding marker diseases like dementia, tuberculosis, and pneumocystis-pneumonia. Doctors tell us that the nonspecific symptoms of night sweats, fatigue, fever, weight loss and diarrhea, are indicative of the presence of HIV in the body prior to so-called full blown AIDS. Yet, these symptoms could very well be indicators of a host of other bodily illnesses. However, if doctors tell a person s/he is going to die, s/he will begin to unconsciously prepare the way for death.

Being diagnosed HIV+ is easier than you think. HIV antibody tests actually test for reaction to proteins, not the presence of an actual virus. Ten proteins are tested for. If the test reveals a reaction to three or four of the proteins tested for, depending the definition of what constitutes an HIV+ diagnosis in that part of the world, you are then said to be HIV+. Further, catch phrases like "full-blown AIDS," "T-cell count," "CD-4," "viral load," and other terms serve to *program* people using a language/lexicon of death; *"cues"* to keep you in a consciousness of fear, a consciousness of shame and guilt over sex and your sexuality. The resulting emotional states brought on by fear lower the body's energetic vibration and lead to physical symptoms of disease.

I implore you to ask yourself the following critical questions:

- "What are HIV antibody tests really looking for?" Certainly they are not looking for a virus that has never been isolated.

- Is it possible that HIV antibody testing is really about *melanin*? Are the tests looking to identify people who are about to experience accelerated spiritual expansion and spiritual ability?
- When the test locates the gene(s) for those traits, are those people targeted for destruction?

My hunch is, "Yes". HIV antibody testing is a sinister agenda for the destruction of *melanated* people of color. It is an attempt to thwart the evolution of human consciousness. My hunch is that somebody knows the power of *melanin*, the black substance from the triple blackness of space; the chemical key to greatness of the black bodies and great minds of organic people who are carbon beings. Somebody wants to keep us from moving from the physical to the spiritual dimension of awareness. Somebody wants to keep Black people and others from knowing who they really are, potential and latent high spiritual beings of great worth. Somebody wants to keep us from our innate dormant potential to change or redirect the weather and talk to the sun. Somebody knows the *metaphysics of consciousness* but thinks that we are not aware of our own power. They are wrong. They do not want us to know or re-member that we are indeed god-beings. Somebody wants to keep us from unlocking all the power and potential in our DNA. Somebody wants to diminish our courage, arrogance and tenacity, and is making an attempt to stop our internal explosions and awakening cellular structure. What is happening inside our bodies is inevitable and is indicative of the shift in consciousness that is happening. It will not be stopped. We will not be stopped. They will not succeed. They will not break the God Code.

They want to take-out *melanin* carriers through the farce of HIV antibody testing and administration of poisonous drugs that literally block the synthesis of DNA.

I believe HIV antibody tests look for certain genetic markers. When the test finds those markers, the person is said to be HIV+ and is then targeted for destruction. People are murdered by the propagation of fear and the administration of prescribed highly-toxic drugs. They are targets for destruction.

***Did you know that selling body parts, especially body parts of *melanated* Black people, is a billion(s) dollar per year industry? I wonder what we would find if we exhumed the bodies of those slain to the HIV Hoax. I would venture to guess: missing organs, body parts sold on the market to make melanin pills? *** Just a thought.

This deception through HIV testing will be stopped. We will not fail. Time will tell. Time has already told. We are onto the fact that something is surely amiss. We already know that something is seriously flawed with the HIV hypothesis, and we are well on our way to finding out who is responsible for this dark agenda. We will not fail.

Any and everybody who after learning the truth of these travesties, yet who continues to be party to them, shall be subject to Divine Retribution.

Until that time, the time of reckoning, I am here to attest to spontaneous healing from physical symptoms of illnesses created by prolonged fear. You too can heal from any disease, including so-called HIV symptoms, and create and maintain a healthy mind, body and spirit, through awareness of the chakras, Kundalini awakening, prayer, meditation, relaxation and spirit guidance. Know that consciousness is really "all there is." Nothing exists, save consciousness.

The ability to be conscious is a form of non-physical energy that extends its influence into matter through the use of biological vehicles. Your body is a vehicle for the expression of consciousness. All that you see outside yourself is a reflection of your consciousness. Accepting that consciousness creates your experiences allows you to choose a consciousness of health.

Healing from so-called HIV theories and deceptions by educating yourself is paramount. Antiretroviral drugs (ARVs) are highly toxic to the body. Those of you who have been identified and diagnosed so-called HIV+ might want to immediately consider refusing to take your prescribed, toxic drugs because they block the synthesis of DNA at the mitochondrial level. Proteins, [e.g., Adenine (A), Thymine (T), Guanine (G) and Cytosine(C)] are the building blocks of DNA and they hold the keys to your connection to the cosmos. Your DNA holds your ancestral memory. In addition, those identified as HIV+ will find it helpful to cleanse the body of toxic drugs through ozone (oxygen) therapy while making dietary changes.

Make no mistake, a hodgepodge of so-called scientific research accompanied by outreach and activist group response to mass hysteria and the resulting miss-education of the public masks the simple truth of disease; that health comes from within. The reason for disease on our planet is because we are not energetically *vibrating* at a level that maintains our original light code. Ignorance of the reality of our existence and negative emotional reactions results in missing and ignoring the very opportunities for which we incarnated. Consequently, there is an imbalance in energy distribution in the body which invariably leads to disease unless corrected.

In truth, there is nothing to be healed, only love for to be revealed. You must therefore let go of your fears and respond with love. Love and acceptance of self must take presence over your fears and selfish, ill-sighted social norms and mores in order to free yourself from unnecessary guilt and shame. These are states of consciousness that draw from the ethers disease-causing agents that manifest as physical ailments and illnesses in the body. Diseases find their victims just as mold finds bread, infection finds wounds, and germs find filth. They proceed from the ethers.

There was nothing in the physical world that comes into existence without having proceeded from the spiritual world. Just as you can make yourself sick pursuant to your beliefs and thought processes, you can also make yourself healthy by releasing shame and guilt over sex and sexuality. I submit to you that when any group of people are degraded and blamed for the ills of society, unity among them is derailed. When the homosexual gatekeepers, shamans and healers of the tribe are not respected, the community tribe suffers.

Know that I will remain on the front-lines doing battle against ignorance. I will conquer it.

Why Sharing This With You Means So Much to Me

This book will teach you the metaphysics of self-healing through chakra and Kundalini awareness. What is that? Stay focused. I will teach you. I will help you learn to restore balance to your energetic system and heal your body.

Today I am free of the physical symptoms of so-called HIV, but I remember the day that I gave them to myself. Yes, you read it correctly. I gave myself bodily symptoms of disease that we typically refer to as being HIV+. At the time, I did not know that so-called HIV might have nothing to do with dying from the HIV/AIDS disease, as we were told at that time.

Perhaps, I was unable and/or unwilling to accept the responsibility that came with the awareness that I created my own physical symptoms and illness from my own prolonged ill-states of consciousness. Somehow, I felt it easier for me to be the victim of circumstance than the creator of my world. The core deception was that it was easier for me to attempt to blame someone else for giving me HIV, rather than accept that I, through my own ill-state of consciousness awareness created physical manifestations of disease in my body.

I literally had to adapt to the truth of the matter that my own ill-states of consciousness had created physical symptoms in my body, in order for me to heal. I was required to change my old ways of thinking by elevating my own consciousness to heal my physical organs. The misimpression was that I was not capable of changing my consciousness and would then have been powerless over my life. However, by embracing my personal power, I liberated my consciousness and propelled my own spiritual evolution.

Desiring to heal every aspect of my life, I took responsibility for my own thoughts, words and actions. I committed to continually seek to become a master balancer of physical reality, emotional tribulation and psychological whirlwinds. I vowed to understand and constantly remind myself that the past is an illusion and that the present is all there is. I surrendered my ego to the spirit of love and emancipated my own consciousness from the limitations of my mind and body. I accepted self-healing.

My work and the research presented in this book will challenge your beliefs about so-called HIV. Further, it is my intent that you begin to see yourself as a powerful creator of your world. You are not a victim unless you choose to be a victim. You can create health in your body if it is diseased. You can go from being *dis-eased* with yourself to being *at-ease* with yourself.

I firmly believe that our Beloved Ancestors (Ankh-estors) are waking us from beyond the veil, leading us to information that will help set us free from the shackles of mental, physical, emotional, and spiritual slavery thrust on us by the so-called elite members of society, many of whose psychopathic nature demonstrates their ill-will toward humanity. I am so grateful for your guidance, your love, and your persistence with me. I hear you. I love you.

Anyone desiring to heal "dis-ease" with self must come to *inner-stand and over-stand* that spontaneous self-healing is possible. Further, a person must realize that s/he can become attuned to nature; his/her own body and the energies of the chakras through meditation, relaxation and spirit guidance—thus creating and/or maintaining a healthy mind, body and soul. You can reintegrate your fragmented soul and be whole again. Accepting that consciousness creates your experiences allows you to choose health. Consciousness is all there is. Nothing else exists.

Let HIV Set You Free

> *"If there is evidence that HIV causes AIDS, there should be scientific documents, which either singly or collectively demonstrate that fact, at least with a high degree of probability. There is no such document."*
>
> Dr. Kary Mullis,
> *Biochemist, 1993 Nobel Prize for Chemistry*

You Are Imprisoned By Non-Science

It is time to re-evaluate the HIV-AIDS hypothesis:

- ❖ Is HIV really the cause of AIDS?
- ❖ Why are scientists still saying that the cause of AIDS is still unknown?
- ❖ Why do the heretics not believe in the so-called virus known as HIV?
- ❖ Why has it not been revealed to the masses of people through the media that HIV was never isolated and that HIV antibody tests are worthless?
- ❖ Why are bio-medical scientists and others still claiming that HIV is not sexually transmitted?
- ❖ Why are scientists saying that people are poisoned to death by toxic antiviral drugs?
- ❖ Why is it that whenever science cannot determine the tangible cause of disease, it relegates its cause to contagion or contraction of some illusive particle that mysteriously (moves) from host to host?
- ❖ *Consider the following: You have been informed that a scientific study has revealed that you are at risk for a particular disease. Further, you are told that it is inappropriate sexual behavior that makes you more susceptible to "contracting" the disease. Next, the religious community begins to claim that God has declared that those behaviors make you a sinner and worthy*

of death. Add to that media reports about homophobic psychopaths who, fearing homosexual tendencies in themselves, physically attack innocent gay people. Imagine the fear that is generated. You can be certain that it will lay the groundwork for unconscious self-created dis-ease. Stress brought on by these types of situations can cause all types of ailments from backache to cancer and cause lowered self-esteem. When the emotions become damned up, anxiety and tension increase, blood and body fluids stagnate and disease sets in. A person becomes dis-empowered and a victim of other people's desires and expectations.

Consider the following non-HIV explanations for AIDS facts taken from an article by Christine Maggiore called, "If it's Not HIV, What Can Cause AIDS?"

- AIDS is a collection of familiar illnesses not a disease.
- Since 1993 more than half of all new AIDS diagnoses in the United States are given to people who are not ill. In 1997, two thirds of Americans diagnosed with HIV had no symptoms or illness.
- Acquired immune deficiency predates the creation of the category "AIDS" and had numerous, well-documented causes.
- There are no AIDS cases noted in the medical literature in which HIV has proved to be the sole health risk factor.
- There are well-documented causes for every AIDS disease that do not involve HIV, and all illnesses now called AIDS occur in the absence of HIV.
- HIV antibody tests do not test for the actual virus, but for anti-viral proteins or genetic material that are not specific to HIV.
- The chance of a positive reaction on a non-specific HIV antibody test increase proportionately with the level of other antibodies and microbes found in the blood.
- Five of the six AIDS risk groups defined by the CDC have health risk factors that involve multiple, chronic exposure

to viruses, bacteria and other antigens known to produce antibodies identical to those associated with HIV.

- Once a person has tested HIV positive, chemotherapy and other immune suppressing chemicals are almost always prescribed for treatment or prevention of AIDS.

- Alternative explanations for AIDS provide opportunities for effective AIDS prevention and for using practical, nontoxic approaches to resolving AIDS (Maggiore, 2007).

You might be surprised to learn that an HIV antibody test is not a test for an HIV virus. The test is a simple test to find certain antibodies in the blood; an HIV antibody test (helpforhiv.com). The proteins used in the HIV antibody test kits have never been proven to be unique or specific for HIV. In fact, every protein used in the test has been found to be associated with conditions that have nothing to do with HIV; and many of these proteins have nothing to do with illness of any kind.

No scientific evidence exists that proves that a positive HIV antibody test means that you have HIV or AIDS. Further, no HIV antibody test, whether it uses blood, urine, or saliva has ever been approved by the U.S. Food and Drug Administration (FDA) for the specific intended purpose of diagnosing infection with HIV. There is even a disclaimer that comes with the test kit that says that the test cannot diagnose actual infection with HIV. For additional information, please go to helpforhiv.com and www.youtube.com/watch?v=6xaM9XwOeY4. I will also offer additional information about the test later in this book.

As of 2010, 34 million people worldwide have been diagnosed HIV+. About one-half of them were women, and 1-tenth children younger than age 15. In the United States alone according to the most recent data from the Center for Disease Control (CDC) 473, 000 had so-called AIDS, not just the so called virus. 76,400 were youths aged

13 to 24. 279,100 were women. 1,148,200 Americans aged 13 and older were living with HIV in 2009 http://www.nichd.nih.gov/health/topics/hiv/conditioninfo/Pages/how-many.aspx.

Women, mostly Black women, are under attack. According to the World Health Organization (WHO), women represent one half of people diagnosed so called HIV+, even higher in Sub-Saharan Africa. In the United States, women make up ¼, with Black women being said to be more than 16 times more likely than white women to be so called infected with HIV http://www.nichd.nih.gov/health/topics/hiv/conditioninfo/Pages/how-many.aspx.

Children are also under attack. An estimated 9000 young people ages 13 to 24 are said to be infected, most of whom are gay or bisexual males and homosexual males. A staggering 200 children younger than the age of 13 were diagnosed HIV+ in 2011 http://www.nichd.nih.gov/health/topics/hiv/conditioninfo/Pages/how-many.aspx.

It is time to awaken to the truth about HIV antibody testing! Stop allowing yourself to be bamboozled and hoodwinked. Many are still allowing themselves to be railroaded into a death campaign for genocide and eugenics. They are being murdered. Their family fabric is being destroyed. They have allowed themselves to buy into a campaign of deceit and destruction without having thought to do the research for themselves and think critically about this crisis.

It is this writer's recommendation that no one ever take an HIV antibody test so that they can avoid the misery, trauma, stress and grief of receiving an HIV+ diagnosis. Instead, if you experience physical symptoms of illness, listen to your body, assess your thinking patterns, release negativity, stop illicit and illegal drug and alcohol use, meditate and relax your body while focusing on the divine in you. Then, claim perfect health. Reconsider before you embark on a toxic drug regimen.

An HIV+ diagnosis can precipitate a spiral towards a death that would otherwise not have happened.

In addition, I implore every reader to empower him or herself by researching the other side of the HIV hypothesis/AIDS crisis for him/herself. By going over the information and resources provided in this book, you will gain an understanding of how and why the idea of HIV is nothing short of a hoax thrust upon innocent minds. In the introduction, I mentioned researchers, scientists and others who believe as I do. In this, book, please refer to Appendix (A) HIV Dissent Resources for an extensive list of resources, or study the Rainbow Warrior Companion at ConsciousDr.com.

The alleged causes of HIV disease being forwarded by corporate doctors and media are killing masses of people. Scientific studies of the HIV virus and pharmaceutical drug issuance and the like are paving the way for death and destruction of human life all over the world. Propagation of fear fuels a consciousness of fear and influences people to become dis-eased and can result in illnesses. The resulting chaos profit's the AIDS Establishment, pharmaceutical companies, corporate medical professionals, and many others. It even provides ways to fuel segments of the world economy. These mass murders are disguised as philanthropy and are attempts to control world populations, as well as thwart the evolution of human consciousness.

If you are a member of the homosexual, lesbian, gay, bi, transgender (LGBT) community please protect yourself my educating yourself about HIV dissent. Sadly, there are those who consider us "undesirables" and "personae non gratae". They desire us dead—especially the Black male homosexuals. I am a Black, Same-Gender-Loving (SGL)/homosexual man who survived and thrived beyond the odds. Close friends of mine did not survive. They are dead. They were slain by the Aids Establishment. They were mere collateral damage of big business.

I removed myself from the prevailing HIV paradigm in 1998. I learned the power of thought. I learned to love myself. But that had not always been the case.

How I Was Set Free

In 1984, I became imprisoned by imaginary walls when a news anchor appeared on television, and announced that homosexual men were developing a sexual disease that could lie dormant in the body for ten to fourteen years. The disease, he said, breaks down a person's immune system leaving the body defenseless against opportunistic infections and that death was imminent. Further, the reporter said that a person could know that the virus had entered the body because two small blisters would appear on the lower leg.

The next day, after a horrible night of worry, I reluctantly examined my lower left leg and there, God forbid, were two small blisters. I immediately rubbed my eyes and looked again to be sure that I was not hallucinating. Was this real, or was I imaging? In horrible fright, I asked myself, "Am I awake or am I having a bad dream?" I thought, "Oh my God I have contracted the HIV virus." I was instantly horrified, petrified and numb.

In a state of frenzy, I reviewed my entire sexual history and convinced myself that I must have contracted HIV from a single sexual encounter I had had about a week earlier from a would-be lover and friend, who had left town just as quickly as he had stolen my heart. Now, in my mind, he had stolen my life. That night as I sat on my bed, I shivered and cried. In disbelief, I could not keep my eyes from returning to the mysterious blisters on my lower leg. Filled with terror and anger, my body began to tense and tremble. My blood curdled. My heart dropped. My mind became frantic and I knew that my life would never be the same. I was forever changed. How could this be? I thought, "I am only nineteen years old. I'll be dead by thirty-three. In fact, I'm dead now. I am a walking dead person. Where do I go? What do I do?"

Even without an HIV positive diagnosis from a doctor at that time in 1984, I had doomed myself to a life of death. The groundwork for unconscious, self-created illness had been planted in me by the talking-head tell-lie-vision news anchor and was to become a sort of self-fulfilling prophecy. I literally thought of myself as among the *walking-dead*. From that day, I became a prisoner of imaginary walls, walls whose suffocating enclosure surrounded me and reminded me that I was worthy of death; a Black, gay, homosexual man who was not fit to live, an abomination, a disgrace to my race and family, a disgrace to myself.

That day, a race ensued, a race towards death, a running from the self and all that I knew as safe and secure up to that point in my life. Drugs and alcohol later ruled my life. They provided temporary relief and comfort. Feigned affection from temporary people and the temporary illusion of love was the only way to deal with the shame and guilt, from a life lived in vain. No more looking in the mirror to see the king I was to become. There was no need to search for the pot of gold at the end of the rainbow. There was only death. In the end, there would be a dilapidated bag of bones, human decay.

I reasoned that the God I knew at that time was punishing me for being a homosexual. I felt I deserved to die. After all, I was called a sissy in childhood. As a teenager, I actually used to practice the way I walk so as to appear more masculine.

I lost the will to be dynamic, a leader. I lost all vision and hope for a bright future. I thought, "Now is the time to prepare for 'Silence

Death,'" a phrase not yet coined at the time. I thought, "This is what you get for choosing to be a homosexual. You're disgusting. You're a faggot. You deserve to die."

My mind was inundated with negative thinking. Fear of the past, present and future set me on a mission to self-destruct. Instead of thinking of life's miraculous opportunities, I spoke of its difficulties, limitations and insurmountable challenges. I lost all zest for living. I lived in a consciousness of self-doubt, self-hatred, extreme shame and debilitating guilt over my sexuality. I lived unenthusiastically and I waited to die.

Prior to receiving my so-called HIV+ diagnosis in 1996, throughout the 14 years since initially hearing about HIV, I had watched friends and associates die and so I forecasted my own impending doom. I also continued to learn all I could about disease and prayed for help and health. Numbness in my fingers and toes were so-called "side-effects" of ingesting my newly prescribed, encapsulated best friends, the drugs Epivir (Lamivudine) and Zerit (Stavudine).

Having to sign the roster at the pharmacy where anyone signing after me could view the log and discover my horrible secret by seeing my name there in plain view along with the names of the drugs I received became almost too much to bear. When I returned home, I even invented a technique for discarding the bottles of HIV drugs with my name on them. I would then transfer to pills into a Kodak film vial and hide the vile in the coat pocket of a green suit that hung in my closet.

Any other person would probably not have been so neurotic and perhaps would have been glad to have a glimmer of hope in a bottle, but not me. For years I asked myself, "Why do you care so much about what others think of you?" I now know that I didn't think much of myself.

9

After 6 months of taking the prescribed drugs, I finally figured out that (Epivir and Zerit) served no purpose other than as encapsulated reminders of my appointment with death. I learned that twice as many people were dying from the effects of HIV/AIDS retro-viral (ARV) drugs than from illness associated with AIDS.

Death is not a "side effect" to be written off as a simple risk or gamble. Death is the **direct effect** from ingesting prescribed toxic drugs for a prolonged period of time.

Even a monthly trip to the pharmacy became a major source of stress. I pretended to be shopping for toothpaste while the line of people waiting at the pharmacy counter got much shorter. Having to sign the roster where anyone signing after me could view the log and discover my horrible secret by seeing my name, there in plain view, along with the names of the medicines I received, became almost too much to bear.

I stopped taking my prescribed toxic drugs after one year back in 1998 when I began to experience numbness in my fingers and toes and occasional jerky body movements. I am so glad that I did.

Today, over 18 years later, I am the living proof that so-called HIV is a lie, a hoax, a grand scheme and form of *modern-day lynching*. I halted the genocide and eugenics campaign against me, yet others continue to be hoodwinked. For that reason, I act to expose the truth about HIV antibody testing. I act to help young, Black, homosexual men and everybody else save themselves from the perils of the prevailing HIV death campaign.

When I stopped taking poisonous ARVs, I sought information on meditation and relaxation and practiced various techniques daily.

One day as I lay outstretched and absorbed in the presence of God, I slipped beyond thought. I somehow, for a moment in time, quelled the chaotic world within and just existed. I felt as if I was engulfed in utter love. I began to feel a miraculous sensation that began in my feet and proceeded up my entire being, as if playing a melody on my body. From the soles of my feet to the crown of my head, the prickly, tingling sensation pervaded my entire body from head to toe. As I lay paralyzed with eyes wide open and tearful, my mouth agape, and in total awe of what had happened, I had the realization that I had been healed of the dreadful dis-ease I had felt in myself for far too long. I knew self-love that I never knew before.

I was baptized as a baby by water, and now, by the fire of *The Holy Spirit.* Thank you, *Mother God.* Two years later after voracious reading and intense research, I learned that I had had a Kundalini Awakening. Life as I once knew it was never again the same.

Be sure to read the chapter on Kundalini in this book.

How You Are Set Free

The manipulation of human consciousness is an attempted imposition on the *Universal Mind of God,* which can lead one to be dis-eased with oneself. Chakras are energy centers in the body that literally generate your physical form. When energy is not able to move freely through your chakras due to negative or fearful thought patterns, illness can result. Negative thinking causes blockages in energy moving throughout the body which can lead to physical manifestations of disease in your body.

In fact, illness is actually a cosmic event and can be seen as a gift from God. The Universe within is letting you know that something in your thinking and consciousness is not as it should and could be. You are not in a consciousness of love, forgiveness of self and others, compassion, and faith and trust in God (*i.e., the Source of All Good*). That *Source* exists at the center of your being waiting to flourish and heal your body. Know that health and self-healing are affected at the level of thoughts and emotions.

Fear not. If this information has come to you, then you are ready to receive it, for when the student is ready, the teacher will come. I am here for you. However, self-healing is a gift you give to yourself. The gift is you.

Doctors search for cures to disease, but healing is a cosmic event. Doctors treat symptoms of disease, but healing comes from within. Healing begins when there is a consciousness of right-thinking, inner-standing, and the underlying causes for energy imbalance are eradicated. It begins by getting in touch with and resolving the psychological and emotional issues connected to *dis-ease with self*. When you realize that you are not separate from God you will know that you cannot be sick. It is your limited conscious awareness of separateness from others and God that creates *dis-ease* with yourself in your consciousness and disease in your body.

Admit that you have felt hopeless and defenseless, not good enough, sinful, unworthy, and that you denied yourself the right to be healthy. In a sense, you unconsciously punished yourself. You are now ready to take responsibility for your health and your life. No longer will you feel that you need attention from others because you are ill. Your sexuality no longer has to be seen by you as bad or dirty. There is no need to punish your genitals. You can free yourself from self-imposed judgment. In fact, right now you can decide to view the act of sex and the expression of intimacy as a most wonderful healing experience given as a gift. You can choose to refuse to deny yourself the freedom to be exactly who you are. From this moment on you will speak of yourself in positive, present-tense affirmations.

Opportunistic infections cannot find you for you are health. Your new awareness will give you a joy for life. You now think for yourself. Contrived, man-made rules cannot affect how you think and feel about yourself. You let go of "Momma's God." Only you decide what is right or wrong for you. You are now aware that you are a *"Spiritual-BE-ING."* Thus, irrational religious doctrines cannot exert undue influence over you.

You even embrace the darker side of your nature along with the lighter side, and release everything that no longer serves you because now you realize that in order to be whole you must accept and love yourself, even the aspects you think are bad. You were once a person who experienced prolonged periods of rigidity and fear. You held back your spirit and excitement for life.

You are now aware that you are the center of your universe. There is no longer the need for you to be manipulative of other people because you are powerful and only desire to control yourself. Attempting to control others can lead to a consciousness of ***"not self"*** and immune-disorders, but now you are in an open frame of mind. *Compassion and forbearance is braided in your DNA.*

Each day, you will become more and more aware that over-expression of negative behaviors lead to energy imbalance in your body and invariably lead to manifestations of disease symptoms in your body, symptoms that have nothing to do with HIV. They are: insecurity, arrogance, conceit, vanity, aloofness, anger, jealousy, rage, possessiveness, blaming others, self-doubt, constant giving in to authority, resisting change, laziness, impatience, excessive worrying, over-sensitivity to the opinion of others, intense erotic fantasies, feelings of being misunderstood, shame, excessive need for sympathy and other less desirable behaviors. You are not perfect but with your new awareness you are perfect as you are. Energy now flows more freely through your chakras because you have raised the frequency of your vibration.

Colloquially stated, *"Be what you is, and not what you ain't, cause if you ain't what you is, then you is what you ain't."* Be who you are. You know that you are here by divine right. You know who you are.

Who are you? You are love in action. You are down-to-earth, grounded, courageous, comfortable in your body, generous, empathetic, compassionate, confident, sensitive, able to cry easily, creative, warrior-like, powerful, faithful, forgiving, spontaneous, loving and loveable. You are a person who knows that as a man thinks in his heart, so he is. You know your healing is already here.

It is now within your power to accept your reality, or to change it. You are aware that the world, if you choose to see it that way, is a safe place. You choose to no longer come under the power of persuasion from media, doctors, or anyone. No one can take your power away from you. You love the skin you are in and know that you are supported by life.

Surprisingly, you now see yourself in every person you meet. They are reflections of you. When you see someone you think you do not like, you simply observe yourself to see if any corrections need to be made in you and not the other person. That person's presence in your life has taught you more about you. There is something about them that is just like you, though you may have previously denied it.

From this moment on, you only share your body with people with whom you have a heart connection; people whose energy vibrates along or above the frequency of your body, because both of you are a loving person in body, mind and spirit. Never again, will toxic people be allowed to bring down your energy level.

You acknowledge that you learned from perceived mistakes, and you now choose to move forward with ease. You are even thankful for the perceived bad times. You will not allow yourself become loud, violent or aggressive, for they are vexations to your spirit and you have adopted a position of harmlessness and no longer live your life reacting out of fear. You are now a demonstration of love in action.

No job or career, material possession, lack, success or failure, or fear of any kind will ever make you feel anything other than complete respect and love for yourself. Nor will you judge any person because of same.

Because you have elevated your awareness, your thinking is no longer inflamed. You now experience the sweetness of life. You release all tension and anger in your mind and in your body because you no longer feel rejected, stuck in the past, deeply hurt, or resentful toward anyone or yourself. You are now free. You see your life ahead with joy and you experience oneness with everything and everyone.

While debates over whether HIV is real continue, you transcend.

You are healed. And so it is.

HIV has set you free!

And Still, I rise. I rise.

"You may write me down in history
With your bitter, twisted lies
You may tread me in the very dirt
But still like dust, I rise."

                            Maya Angelou

I rise when rejected, stigmatized and vilified. I rise when people claim that homosexuality is a curse. I rise when death tolls go up and my name is on the waiting list to die from a non-existent virus. I rise to teach people who do not want to learn. I rise to help dying friends who refuse to accept the truth about HIV antibody testing. I rise to feed and clothe the homeless, sometimes in my own home. I rise when doctors would rather kill me slowly and profit in the process. I rise to teach and counsel school children who are abused physically, emotionally and sexually. I rise to support friends. I rise when slandered by heterosexuals and homosexuals. I rise when my friends and associates die from toxic drugs. I rise when folk say I am mentally-disordered, a demon, and am going to Hell for being homosexual. I rise daily to carve out a place for myself in a culture and society that thinks the world would be a better place without my kind. I rise every time life attempts to knock me down. And still I rise. I rise. I rise.

You can too. Be a Rainbow Warrior!

Now, why would anyone willingly endure such trauma? Why would a person risk his life to expose the truth about HIV? Because somebody has to stand up and tell the truth about HIV without fear of losing their reputation or career opportunities. Somebody has to do what few are willing to do for the sake of humanity.

I have long-grown tired of being ashamed for being a homosexual Black man. I decided, "No more". Hopelessness and despair left me feeling lonely, as if I only belonged on the outskirts of society, and led me to do many desperate and perhaps irresponsible things. Hopelessness and despair suppressed my immune system because of my beliefs about how society rejects homosexuals—that is, until I allowed doctors to suppress it with toxic drugs. If you ever walked in my footsteps or similar ones you would surely understand.

Sometimes you do not get to know the answers to all of life's questions, but you do get to experience the fruits of forgiveness of self and others. You do get to see how everybody benefits from self-acceptance and the acceptance of others as they are. You sometimes get the chance to see some of the fruits of your hard labor. You do come to learn who you are and who you are not. You do get the opportunity to respect your body-temple. You do get the opportunity to understand disease (dis-ease with oneself) by using your illnesses as a road map to health. You can come to know universal love for all that exists in creation. You get a glimpse of yourself in and through others. You come to understand the power of your own thoughts, words, and actions and come to know yourself as a creator. You do learn compassion for those less fortunate than you. You also see the temporal and transitory fulfillment of material possessions of those you perceive as more fortunate that you. You do come to love those who hate you. You come to understand the illusion and deception of illegal drug use and abuse. You come to accept and love all aspects of your unique self. You can thrive even when others do not want you to be among the living. You come to know God as being in you, everywhere and evenly-present. You can learn to let go and let God. Why? Because it is your divine birthright to be healthy.

No matter what happens in your life, you can decide to free yourself to live in the present moment of awareness, rather than allowing your or others' past, present or future actions to dictate who you are.

Know, however, that there are those who would suggest that you should be ashamed of yourself and your life. The god in you knows differently. Forgive yourself and others. Do not be convinced that you have to live a prudish lifestyle to be acceptable in God's eyes or to receive the blessing of healing.

Bring light into the dark areas of your life. Now, it is time for you to thrive. Now, it is time for you to integrate all of aspects of yourself into a fully functioning person who is wholly healthy.

My Life

My Life is a beautiful expression
Of life's painful lessons
Cryptic confessions
My soul and my word
Remain my only possessions
Amidst the hatred I am sweating
And tears I might leak

My eyes tell a story
Like my feet
A million bottles ran through
Yet my virtue stays true
Like the color of my skin
When it's hot I'm darkening
Six shades and 7 hues
36 moons of dues
My path was chosen
I ain' choose
Just accepted
Divinely selected
To get Truth erected
And even though I'm humble
I'm never copacetic within my blocks of hell
So I keep anger under my fingernails
Like dirt from 40 acres
With my trusty tool of change
Cyber-connection long-range
Clean mud
Dirty rain
Shape shifting through life's lanes
The biggest lie is that I'm lame
~Original poetry by An anonymous friend & Damian
Laster aka Kbr Amen RA Horakhty (2000)

The Healing Process

Help is on the Way

> *"The best kept secret in medicine is that under the right conditions the body can heal itself. Dr. Michael Greger"*

C ontinue to refuse to give life in your mind to the thought of physical death. It is your perception of things you learned as a child about religion that are killing you. That kind of thinking is creating your existence. It is creating your experiences. All the religious dogma, fear, guilt and shame are killing you and you do not have to allow that anymore.

Refuse to search for what is and will always be right where you are. No longer allow any negative thought to have power over you. Any thought of illness, lack, fear, jealousy, envy, or anger is to be dismissed. Take control of your thinking. "All-Good" is your new motto. Everything that happens to you is "all-good". There might actually be something events or circumstances that appear to be adversary. But in your mind it is all good. Your salvation is a free gift and from now on you accept the gift of self-healing with thanks and praise.

This is perhaps the greatest and most profound lesson for you and all humanity to learn: *nothing else exists but (love); all power, all knowledge, everywhere, evenly present.* There is no room for anything else except in one's own mind, which exists in every cell of the body and not just in the brain as we've been misled to believe.

All these revelations ring true in your whole body. They reverberate in your bones. They vibrate in your being. How could you have been so gullible to believe that God doesn't love you because you are homosexual, a supposed sinner?

Prior to my healing (described in Chapter one), I decided that what I needed was time away from the world and everything and everyone in it; time to free myself from the contaminated thinking and conditioning of life in this physical plane of existence. Could I stop judging others and myself? Could I come to love myself just as I am?

I turned off the tell-lie-vision, radio and telephone ringer. No outside influence or interference was allowed in until the *Christ in me* was made manifest. I learned to meditate merely by seeking that knowledge.

"Om Namah Shivaya" became my mantra. I honor the "Christ" potential in me.

The universe began to bring all I needed for healing into my life. By going inside myself, I met the presence of divine love where *IT* existed—deep within my heart and core of my being. There, I communed in earnest.

I prayed fervently day and night until healing happened. Somehow, I knew that complete healing was waiting for me. I just did not know exactly how my healing would happen. The timing was totally unexpected. I had no idea what healing was all about, until I received it.

"As I lay outstretched in absolute thanks and praise to God for all of me, it was as if I had slipped beyond thought and just existed. Somehow, for a moment in time I quelled the chaotic world within. Without warning, I began to feel a miraculous sensation beginning in my feet and proceeding up my entire being as if playing a melody on my body. I honestly felt like a holograph of myself. I could not move. I did not want to move. What was happening to me? From the soles of my feet to the crown of my head, the prickly tingling sensation pervaded my entire being. I lay, as if paralyzed, with my mouth agape and tearful eyes, in total awe at what had just happened. And then came the realization that I had been healed of the dreadful

dis-ease I had felt of myself for far too long. I had been given an opportunity to know self-love as I never had before. After two years of intense research, I realized that the grace of God had descended on me, at birth by water and now by the fire of the Holy Spirit. I learned that I had had a Kundalini Awakening." --Damian Q. Laster aka Kabir Amen RA Horakhty (The Rainbow Warrior: Healing HIV through Chakra Awareness, 2001)

Yet, I had accumulated so much baggage from misguided affection, illegal drug use, lies and general running from the self. I continued run from me. While my body was healed, I now needed healing for my fragmented soul.

How could I reintegrate all of myself, my fragmented personality and lost will to live? Could I keep ahead of scientific research reports, news media, societal norms and beliefs and self-imposed negativity? Would happiness, abundance and peace become my natural state of mind?

I decided to love myself, just as I am.

I decided to share this most precious information with you, even though I was fearful of being rejected and being considered insane. I did not want to be thought of as a fool or as a spreader of disease. I was not a degreed medical scientist. Who was I to challenge the medical profession and claim that I knew about HIV, general disease in the body and physical symptoms of disease?

I thought, "Are you really going to reveal all the dirt of your life and tell everybody your personal business?" Then I thought, "My body will return to the dirt of the earth just as I was fashioned from it by *Supreme Creator*, but my soul will rise, because soul is eternal. The dirt of my life is that which propelled will rise because my the truly inspiring Iyanla Vanzant, who said, *"There is value in the valley."*

I realized through the chain of events in my life that I must spread the message of healing as I had experienced it to all my brothers and anyone who would listen.

Many are suffering after having been diagnosed so-called HIV+, and are dying from fear and prescribed toxic drugs. Fear is the deadliest killer. Those who are willing to perhaps consider a new way of approaching life and this crisis can certainly benefit from my story of healing. I represent the *One* who healed me. I represent me. I represent self-healing through awareness of self as a vessel of *The Most High God*.

I encourage others to choose health and life just as I did. Choose to experience divine love and comfort. I was chosen to share the message of divine love and self-healing with you and I am up for the task. I do what all *Rainbow Warriors* are called to do. Our efforts shall not be in vain.

This book offers a wealth of information for you to examine your own thought patterns so that you will choose to work on accepting healing just as I did. Know that your body is a god-technology, and was designed to heal itself. You have just forgotten this and/or have been falsely led away from the awareness that you, in concert with divine love, have this most powerful ability—the ability to heal yourself. You have powers beyond your immediate knowing. Look no further than within yourself.

Metaphysician, Heal Thyself; Radiate and Spiral

> *"The real challenge (in life) is to choose, hold, and operate through intelligent, uplifting and fully empowering beliefs."*
> -Michael Sky

How do you meet this challenge? Let go of Momma's God and get to know *Mother God, Goddess Kundalini/Holy Spirit*. Negotiate fear with love. Create purpose for your life. Heal family ties if possible. Establish reliable relationships. Learn of the chakras. Meditate. Practice relaxation. Listen to your inner guides, teachers and angels, pray, think critically, think positive, surrender all your perceived problems and see the wonders of the universe.

Again, please know that if this book has come to you, then you are ready to receive the information presented herein. Love is expressing through me. I am in no way claiming to be able to reveal love to anyone, for only love can do that—the love within you. Use this information to heal yourself and others of *physical symptoms* of any disease, more accurately understood as (dis)-(ease) with yourself. If you experience physical symptoms, know that they have nothing to do with a never before purified and isolated so-called HIV virus. Your physical symptoms are a result of prolonged fear, worry, shame and guilt. Your symptoms of disease are self-created and as such can be self-healed when you decide to heal the underlying causes that created them; ill-states of consciousness.

Healing your soul is a spiritual matter and is of great significance. My message to you is only one in the evolution of information available to us, as we all begin the new millennium seeking to become a highly-evolved spiritual beings.

This book offers mental causes for physical illnesses and metaphysical ways to overcome them. Have faith in the process and know that you are loved just as you are. Know that you are healed right now. Healing and restoration of health just needs to manifest in your body.

Start by asking yourself a series of questions:

- Do I believe in my heart that when I have homosexual encounters I am doing something wrong?
- Do I feel ashamed and guilty about having sex?
- Do I experience feelings of self-hate because I yield to homosexual desires?
- Do those I love think that I am going to hell for being homosexual?
- Am I able to sustain loving relationships?
- Do I stay in relationships because I want to reduce the number of people I have sex with, thereby reducing my chances of contracting the so-called HIV virus?
- Is sex a dirty act?
- Am I in the closet because I am ashamed of being homosexual?
- Have I ever spoken harshly of other homosexual people or myself because of their expression of their sexuality?
- Do I experience bodily tension when I hear about HIV/AIDS, have sex or think about having sex?

If you answered, yes to any one of those questions, know that you are at risk for creating physical symptoms of illness in your body.

The most important question to ask yourself is: *Am I Christ-like?* If you are not, you can work on all aspects of your being and your personality. Perhaps it is you who needs to change.

Next, ask yourself if you are willing to do the mental work necessary to forgive yourself for patterns of thinking that can cause you bodily harm? Do you believe that there is no dis-ease that cannot be healed? Are you worthy of a life of health and happiness just the way you are? Have you realized that every illness presents you with the opportunity to learn life lessons and stimulate spiritual growth? Are you able to free yourself to think for yourself?

If you answered yes to any of these questions, you are on your way to self-healing.

Consider that healing involves getting in touch with and resolving the psychological and emotional issues connected to disease (dis-ease with oneself). Now, consider that you needed the disease to teach you more about yourself and about *who you really are;* a spiritual being having a physical human experience. Now imagine that all you have to do is reconnect and surrender to love.

Disease or dis-ease with self is equated to cells that have died or are dying, or deliberately killed by other cells. However, upon receiving healing and on the path to your spiritual ascension, all cells that have died or are dying are resurrected into crystalline form. All cells receive a new blueprint that is supportive rather than destructive to the overall health and wellness of your physical form. *"This is the gift of ascension, an ageless disease-free form that can live to see a new era of peace and unity for humanity and Earth." (The Great White Buffalo, The Earth Mother, channeled through Karen Danrich, 1998-2001)*

Thoughts that you hold in your mind and words you speak create your experiences. You have merely learned through false conditioning to hate or suppress parts of yourself. You can also unlearn and relearn. You can begin to love every part of yourself and re-experience health in your body. If you become ill in any way, you can uncover the ill thinking pattern that created the physical, bodily manifestation of disease, acknowledge it, change it and re-experience health: for all dis-ease is rooted in ill-thinking.

Authors like Louise L. Hay and many other authors have written about healing, metaphysics and spirituality. I have included a list of many of those authors and their books in Appendix (B) of this book. I highly recommend that you investigate them as you continue your spiritual journey.

Begin to practice asking yourself in every moment of every day, is this thought, will these words, will this action bring about joining or separation? Feelings and emotions of separation from self or from others can lead to ill health.

There is nothing wrong with having sex. Homosexual men and women are not wicked because of their sexuality; they are as are other people, wanting of love. There is nothing wrong about being homosexual, bisexual, or transgendered. Stop believing the lies. You are perfect as you are. You are you. Your life is unfolding right now. God loves you just the way you are. God is love, however expressed. All else is illusion. There is no need to change your sexuality unless you decide that it is your desire to do so. You are made in God's image and are perfect just the way you are. In fact, you are God expressed in a physical form. You are a direct expression of God.

There is no religious doctrine, law or teaching that should keep you from knowing that fact. You are in a process of remembering who you really are. You are direct expressions of the *Source* that created *Itself* in infinite variety. The *Supreme Creator* made you perfect as you are. You must only admit that you already know that in your heart. You must re-member.

Many refuse to accept this truth. They insist on seeing themselves as separate and removed; on seeing themselves as sinners because others have told them that their sexuality makes them sinners. Sin, a word originating in the sport of archery means to "miss the target."

Many feel or perceive that they have missed the target and did not accomplish what God asked of them. Sin is any "thought" that turns us away from love. It actually is anything that cuts you off from love and causes suffering.

You can never cut yourself off from divine love. Love is really all there is in the universe. All else is an illusion. You are loved regardless of deed. If you feel that what you are doing is a misdeed, it is your suffering that can guide you back toward the right-action of loving yourself. Doing so, in turn, alleviates suffering and refocuses your eye on the divine within your mortal self.

You are called to love yourself completely despite any "thing" you might do. There is "no-thing" you could do to stop you from loving yourself. Yet, you continue to cut yourself off from divine love. Can you not cease with the hypocrisy and begin to love yourself? The most important message you could ever receive is that is that you are loved infinitely. Love indwells you. You can and must, however, always continue to evolve from your status in the universe into beings of divine worth. You are that potential, given the spark of love that resides in you.

Cease feeling separate from God and others. You are one with the *Creator.* You have been given life to create and experience. Serve yourself and others. Never blame life or other people for what you have created, even your illnesses. Your illnesses serve the purpose of teaching you more about yourself and provide an opportunity for you to learn to be all that you can be.

No, no one gave you HIV. There is no sexually transmitted HIV virus. No one can give you cancer. No one but you can make you ill. No one can think for you but you. You get what you create, just as I got what I created—physical symptoms that I was at "dis-ease" within my own self. This is a simple truth, the acknowledgment of which can restore your physical health.

Now you can take full responsibility (response-ability) for your own health. You can stop feeling guilty and ashamed for being you. You can stop giving away your personal power to others who might rather see you dead. You can embrace all that you are and not have to hide. You can embrace others like you without all the division within our homosexual communities and within the human community. You can truly come to know the meaning of love and see it as a reality in your world. You can let go of fear, doubt, worry, guilt, shame, jealousy, anger and despair.

I was once diagnosed with a form of conjunctivitis (pink-eye). The doctor couldn't tell me how I got it, or figure out how to cure it. Surprisingly, at that time, nothing he said or did had a healing effect on me. He admitted to me that he had no cure for my form of pink eye. Yet, he said it was highly contagious and could be a serious illness. Having already experienced healing from so-called HIV, I knew that I could use meditation to uncover my ill thoughts and reveal what in my thinking was causing me to feel that my life was not as it should be. I wisely realized that I was angry and frustrated at what I was "seeing" in life. I was frustrated with my job and the people I encountered daily at work. To heal myself, I went within during meditations and reconnected with the loving flow of divine energy. I began to *"see"* through eyes of love. I accepted that there was no situation in my life that would not be remedied with love. Within three days, with love realization, I healed myself.

Taking full responsibility for all you do and think requires a huge commitment from you to learn the lessons from the consequences of choices made which resulted in illness. Self-healing is about assessing your inner potential to recover and perform at an optimal level on the path to achieve your highest aspirations. You must breathe more spirit into your mind, body, and emotions, while releasing tension and negativity, and gain access to your deepest essence.

Since your body contains the blueprint for self-healing, your spiritual task in this lifetime is to learn to balance the energies of your body, emotions, mind and your soul. Understanding the chakras as energy centers vertically aligned along the spine that run from the base to the crown of the head, you gain more personal and spiritual power when you ascend from embodiment of the lower chakras to enlightenment of the upper chakras.

A Wounded Healer

I have become the doctor that I always wanted to be as a child. I am a metaphysician, urban shaman and healer, a twin-spirited gatekeeper. I guard the gates between worlds. I heal myself and help others learn of their ability to heal themselves. I am a wounded healer.

Can you be bold enough to claim goodness in every aspect of your life, or will you continue to live a life in fear of any and everything your mind can concoct? Will you continue to allow others to lead you to hate yourself? Are you capable of demanding and claiming self-respect? Yes, you most certainly are capable. Know that love and respect will follow from others?

I thank Father-Mother God for using illnesses to remind me of the *Christ-potential* within me. I am grateful that I have realized and made real a new way of thinking and being in the world.

Who am I? *I AM Who I Am. I Am That I Am. I Am Peace. I Am Love. I Am Joy. I Am Rich. I Am One With The Holy Spirit. I Am One With*

The Universal Mind. I Am One With All Life Forms And They Are One With Me. I Am One With All That Is. I Am Health. "I Am Light. I Am as God Is.

In fact, whenever I use the phrase *"I Am,"* I speak it in an uplifting and positive manner that carries all the power of love from the *Source of All That Is.* Never speak your "I Am" presence in a negative manner. "I am" is your connection to divine love and can never be anything short of the fullness of that love.

The contents appearing here represent a calling to recognize that illness is a gift from the cosmos. It provides a way of alerting you to your sense of separation in consciousness awareness. You are never alone. *Supreme Creator* never leaves you. Now you can truly say thank you to *Father/Mother God* for helping you see that you can move your thoughts back to love for yourself and others. You can now flourish having been awakened to the truth of who you are. If you would but listen to your body and find your way back to the fullness of divine love, you can re-experience health.

How then do you do this? Begin seeing your body symbolically. The functions of your body- parts represent their connection to your thought processes, which produce your experiences. In other words, your consciousness creates your experiences here in the school known as Earth.

Behold, The Body Electric!

> *"The Body Is A God Technology. It is always In the process of healing itself"*
>
> ~Damian Laster

33

Everything is energy. Simply stated, Einstein's famous formula ($E=mc^2$) tells us that all matter is slowly vibrating energy. The human body with all its structures, organs, tissues, fluids, etc. is made up of cells which are made up of molecules, which are made up of atoms, which are made up of atomic particles, electrons orbiting around their nuclei. Even the atomic particles are made of even smaller sub-atomic particles, quarks and such, which can be described as vibrations of energy. These vibrations of energy are electrical and emanate from the creative force we know as *Source Energy* in action.

The kingdom of heaven is within you. The human mind, body, and spirit are renewed and revivified by *Source Energy*. Healing comes from *Source* energy. Simply acknowledging and allowing it to move unencumbered through you is enough to bring about total recovery from any illness.

Thoughts that you hold in your mind create your experience. Ill-thinking can lead to dis-ease with self, or disease in your body brought on by negative emotions and resulting energy imbalance in your chakras. Participating in your own recovery from disease is not only advantageous but essential to your healing. Rather, than medicating and attempting to block your physical symptoms that are signposts to healing illness, you can self-heal them by realigning your consciousness and your chakras.

Behold the Body Electric! Hands hold life's experiences. Eyes represent the capacity to see the past, present and future clearly. Feet carry you through life and represent your understanding of yourself and others and life. Your stomach digests ideas and holds nourishment. Your heart is your center of love and security. Your lungs breathe in life. Your back supports you through life. Your throat is the center of expression, and so forth. Should you experience problems with any of these body parts, you can then link that bodily disruption to your self-created ill-thinking patterns. Then you can adjust them by healing the thought patterns. When you become your best self, you thus heal your body.

Healing is effected at the level of thoughts and emotions. For example, a person with repressed feelings of anger that s/he is unable to express, might experience chronic constipation along with feelings of depression. When a person comes to grips with feelings of anger and recognizes that they are part of human nature, s/he can then release the guilt over having those feelings. When you release ill feelings and forgive yourself, you can find security in "letting go," thereby relieving the body of constipation, without laxatives.

In some instances, creating illness might be used by you to gain the attention of others or to exert control over them. Be honest with yourself about this if it is a pattern in your behavior. Certain cases of asthma attacks are examples of this phenomenon.

A person experiencing ulcers has issues with fear and anger, usually stemming from a strong belief that they are not good enough. Vomiting might signify a violent rejection of ideas or fear of the new. Venereal disease (VD) typically indicates sexual guilt and can result in the need for unconsciously punishing the genitals because you feel that the genitals are sinful or dirty and that you have been sinful or dirty. Manifestations of cancer and tumors might be reflective of long-standing resentment and carrying deep secrets and/or grief eating away at the self.

How is it that so-called HIV symptoms would rock the entire body and kill in such a vicious way? Fearful thinking attacks the immune system in the body, which serves as its defense mechanism. So-called HIV symptoms develop when a person feels defenseless and hopeless. It thrives when there is a strong feeling of not being good enough, resulting from a denial of the self. These feelings arise when there is sexual guilt and/or shame for being homosexual/Same Gender Loving (SGL). If every SGL person could feel themselves a part of the universal design of life, both powerful and capable of loving and appreciating all aspects of themselves and others, there would be no dis-ease with self.

If you experience a sense of shame and guilt after orgasm, be honest about it. Know that you are not alone. Although there is a feeling of ecstasy, there is often a feeling that you have done something wrong and are a bad person for experiencing sex in this way because of your conditioning. You might not have even been with another sexually, but merely thought of it during the act of masturbation and experienced guilt. Well, now is the time to reconsider sex, which is a most miraculous healer that was given to you as a gift.

Where the mind goes the body will follow. Thought produces energy, and energy follows thought. Thought patterns are simply energy that maintains the frequency of the human personality. Become attuned to the energy of your higher self and experience health.

Some people tend to think of health only in terms of the physical body. The emphasis in western/allopathic medicine is always on the physical examination. Begin to give attention to the subtle spiritual aspects your existence. There is increasing evidence that there is not a physical illness known to science that is not affected by your thoughts and feelings. It is your attitudes and e-motions (energy-in- motion) that play a significant role in your ability to recover from dis-ease. You have allowed yourself to become fearful and doubtful. As a homosexual, you perhaps have denied yourself the freedom to *be*. You sometimes do not nurture your divine right to be and to experience intimacy.

Remove judgment from your sexual expression. It is from the suppression of sexuality that various phobias and hysteria arise and plague societies. Stimulation of erogenous areas on the physical body sends the necessary blood flows to seats of consciousness, activating the personality and increasing the life force through the body, allowing the blood to flow with greater ease. The act of orgasm itself can cause all the chakras to open and heal the body.

People with so-called HIV and AIDS *"symptoms"* also suffer from diarrhea, dementia, carpal tunnel syndrome, diabetes, inflammation, infections, depression, bipolar disorder, manic-depression, lymphoma, and headaches. Each bodily dysfunction can be jointly and severally linked to issues of fear, irritation and anger, rejection and hopelessness. A person manifests bodily illness because of his/her refusal to deal with the world as it is. There is an inability to speak up for one's self because of swallowed anger, struggle and distrust in the process of life; along with self-criticism stemming from the injustices to which one perceives s/he has become victim. It is as if the person cannot assimilate the erroneous information flooding the mind. Joy of life is then lost, leaving the person incapable of having a sense of peace. The "sweetness of life" is no more. At that point, so-called opportunistic infections which are rarely seen in those with normal immune systems, invade the dis-eased body and become deadly.

Do not allow the vultures to scavenge your remains. Accept your divine right to attract individuals that you consciously choose into your life. This allows your personality to flow along natural lines of sexuality which become the balance point from which your individuality flows forth. Denying your sexuality can kill you. Living a life filled with fear paralyzes you.

Sexuality is the attraction between two like-minded individuals according to certain karmic patterns to be expressed in this lifetime. Your personality is shaped by these patterns upon the level of both the soul and the mind. It is shaped by the immediate environment of this particular lifetime, and you attract and/or repel people and circumstances into and out of your life according to natural polarities and magnetic influences. For truly, life is but a series of highly coordinated vibrations. The gift of sexuality is one of the most healing and enlightening of all activities built into the human race. It opens a direct connection to your higher self.

Never sacrifice your in-born desires to contrived man-made rules; instead, the more you live this life as directed by your soul and the divinity within you, the quicker you unfold your human potential. It is not nor ever was intended that we live our lives in bondage to man-made restrictions.

Let go of your fears. Live your life to the fullest. Enjoy your body. Love yourself. Love others. The more you are aware of this truth, the more you open your mind to its higher resources, restore your own angelic nature and become an infinite being: for there is no way to become more, by being made less.

Consider the two emotions of life from which all others are derived: love and fear. Love is the e-motion (energy in motion) that uplifts. It embraces all that is. It conquers all that ever will be. Its quality is one of acceptance. It is the energy that expands all that it touches. Love opens up and sends out. Love soothes and amends. Love stays, reveals, and heals. Love shares. Love allows. It is the ultimate-shareable-emotion and universal-unifying-force. Fear, on the other hand, stands in direct opposition to love. It is the e-motion (energy in motion) that pulls down. Fear refuses to hold and embrace. It rejects. Fear closes down, leaves, makes ill and kills.

These emotions nevertheless are necessary opposites of each other. One does not come to know love without the experience of fear. It is for this reason that whenever one has fearful thoughts they should be carefully examined, acknowledged for what they are and smothered with love. The fear monster must be hit on its head every time it presents itself and demolished for the lie that it is. The dark room must be filled with light, as it were. Fear hinders the flow of energy, while love increases it. Divine love has the power to restore ease to a dis-eased body when we consciously release the fear programs that have been ingrained in us since birth.

One thing that we as humans do is to try to suppress or hide qualities that we feel reveal the darker side of our personalities. We think that if we can only push them back or down inside of ourselves, that they will simply disappear and not bother us. This is the road that leads to illness. It must be *understood, inner-stood and over-stood* that you must be willing to accept all aspects of yourself, the perceived good and perceived bad. Not being yourself, who you were made to be, could cost you your health and possibly your life.

To better conceptualize this concept, take as an example, the perceptions of hot and cold which are only varying measures of temperature. When you perceive that you are doing something wrong, it is just that you have chosen a perception that you have given meaning to in your own mind. More often than not, your perceptions of what is right or wrong are largely based on what society or others tell you. Many times this is done under the guise of religious doctrine and dogma. Others tell you that you *"should"* or *"should"* not do a certain thing, or that you *"should"* behave in a certain way, lest you be damned to hell.

Are you aware that in some African cultures there is no word in their language for *"should"*? Either there is, or there is not. Either you are divine as you are, or you are not.

Remember that you are loved, utterly. There is nothing that you could possibly do to keep love from you. It is only through your thinking that you feel cut off from loving yourself. Only, you choose

39

to look away, because you feel you have done something wrong and are unworthy of receiving divine love.

Know Thyself! Heal Thyself.

Who knew that what I had initially been taught as a child under a patriarchal system, which wrote the *Divine Feminine* out of history and away from prominence and which represented the *Holy Trinity as The Father, Son and Holy Spirit*, was more correctly represented as *Father God, Mother God and The Child of God*? The dual aspect of both the Masculine and Feminine Principles had been intentionally misrepresented in favor of forming a Patriarchy.

The truth is that I was baptized at birth by water, and now by the *Fire of the Holy Spirit/Divine Feminine/Goddess Kundalini*. You can be too.

It is you who can decide if you are unhappy with your creations. It is you who can choose again to create something different. If you are ill or become ill you can choose health. If you are poor you can choose abundance. If sad, choose to be happy. Cease punishing yourself for living your life as you have chosen. Stop listening to others who tell you that you are wrong for being who we are. Remember, the only reason we are here is to (re-member) *who we really are*. What we are, in truth, are divine expressions of love. We are the difference that love makes in the world.

In this light, you can embrace the dark side of your own personality as well as that of others. You can embrace the shadow side of yourself, if you will. All of creation was manifested from the sacred void (darkness). Only then can you flood it with love and bring light into the dark room, bring warmth into a cold room, see sunshine where there was rain, experience peace where there was chaos. In this way, you can reintegrate all of your personal aspects with love. You can appreciate and be uniquely who you are. You will be remembering who and why you are.

Recognize that it is in the pushing down of loving aspects of yourself that blockage in the flow of energy in your "body" is created, which results in disharmony within. Humans are energy beings, as all else in the universe, forever moving and changing.in a perpetual state of motion.

You can learn to relax on the axes of the "wheels" of life through daily meditation. *The Human Body Chakras are the Wheels of Life.* In the next chapter, I will discuss the Human Body Chakra System.

The Chakras, HIV, and AIDS Dis-ease

The Human Body Chakra System

Luxor Temple – "The Temple in Man"

"Teach the great what is useful to them."—Imhotep

    The Temple of Luxor reveals the "The Temple in Man" and the spiritual centers (chakras) in the human body. You will learn that all knowledge proceeded from the progenitors of culture and civilization in Kemet, "The Land of The Black". Your ankh-estors knew about the chakras and the secrets and power of melanin. The Temple of Luxor was a tool they used to keep their vibration and status as high spiritual beings for as long as they possibly could. They knew that they were falling in density into physicality. They knew that pursuant to the Universal Law of Rhythm, what goes up must come down. They also wisely knew that the time would come when we would ascend in consciousness again to take our place as high spiritual beings. The Temple of Luxor reveals the chakras written in stone on the temple walls.

C hakras represent the *"wheels of life"*. They are the energy centers in the body that link us to every living entity and the *Creator*. At this point, let us turn from our image of the *Supreme Creator* as a person figure, and begin to think in terms of the force and presence from which all else stems: *The All*. Through chakra meditation we find God, the **g**ift of **d**ivinity, which lies at the very core of our very being. Chakras are the Primordial Gods on Earth; Nut, Geb and Shu in bondage, so to speak, in the body as chakras.

*You are a (g)od (**g**enerator, **o**perator, **d**estroyer).*

Many are not aware that they are aware of the core energy of chakras. The chakras are nevertheless the still-points of your existence. Chakras are the hubs around which the wheels of light energy revolve, sustaining your physical form. As structural blueprints, serving as conduits for compliment energy information held in higher self, chakras are the interface point between your physical and non-physical form.

Every time you have seen the symbol of the caduceus, the winged staff with two snakes entwined that erroneously represents the medical field, you have come into contact with an aspect of the chakras. As the two headed serpent winds up the staff and intertwines, each point of intersection is symbolic of one of the major chakras of the body. The snakes represent the polarity of opposing forces in nature and the wings illustrate transformation and freedom. There are many chakras in the body, but for our purposes here, the seven major divine portals will be discussed.

Working with the chakras you can begin to open to Spirit and come to better understand who and what you are, what you feel and how you think, change and grow. Through the chakras you can begin to understand how your thinking affects how you relate to self, others and the world. You can then begin to understand how your perceptions of reality affect your thinking patterns and your resulting health.

This book offers only a surface perspective about the Chakras and Kundalini. No spiritual practice is to be taken lightly. Inquire and study before beginning any spiritual practice.

As stated previously, you are an energy being and the chakras are energy centers that draw energy in from the universal energy field and distribute it throughout the body. The chakras are the template for perfection providing a blueprint along which the mind then enters and establishes a correct pattern for itself. You are your subtle energies and they are the roots of your consciousness. As creators and maintainers of your very existence, the chakras hold the key to spiritual awakening, psychological and physical health. Chakras mediate all energy coming into and going out of the body. See chakras as the union of Spirit and matter manifested as consciousness. Chakras are always open since they represent a union of spirit and matter manifested as consciousness. However, any consciousness that is not properly aligned, will disrupt and block the flow and of energy. Although chakras may never be closed, they may become blocked. The resulting energy imbalance can lead to illness. Imbalance in energy affects the mind and the body. The e-motional (energy in motion) and the physical are connected, and if not functioning

harmoniously can begin to wreak havoc on the health and well-being of a person.

A person affected by so-called HIV+ symptoms has without a doubt suffered from emotional imbalance. There have most certainly been prolonged periods of fear, rigidity, restriction of life expression and holding back of the spirit, of excitement in life. Confusion in life resulting from the denial of self can cause one to develop addictions, sexual obsessions, impulsive and reckless behaviors, possessiveness, insecurity and immediate gratification of urges. One would be prone to manipulative behaviors, have power concerns and consequently immune disorders. Feelings of being defenseless against society's judgments of one because of sexual behavior and life-style choices can leave one feeling thwarted and devoid of self-dignity.

Be a Rainbow Warrior.

Whoever assigned the "rainbow" as the gay symbol was a genius, for it has the ability to serve as a cue each time you see it to love yourself. The designer of the symbol must have known that the rainbow colors serve as a bridge to health. They must have had understanding of the chakras and their relation to the visible spectrum of light (photons), namely the colors of the rainbow: (red, orange, yellow, green, blue, indigo, and violet). It is said that *we descended from heaven to earth along the rainbow.*

In those of higher spiritual development, the collection of electromagnetic energies of varying densities in the form of colors of light are seen to revolve at great speed, thus revealing our human aura. Your health, balance and Spirit energy are reflected in these colors. Extending 2 to 5 feet from the body, the colors, textures and patterns of light reveal much information about the physical, emotional, mental and spiritual states of an individual. Every color and shade in the rainbow is present in the aura, and each color of the rainbow corresponds to a chakra in the body from root to crown. The aura reflects the energy of spirit in matter. One can use color therapy during meditation (discussed later) to help align the chakras when there are blockages or holes in the aura. Dramatic changes in the colors of the aura are evident when illnesses occur.

The seven major chakras of the body, their corresponding colors, elements and key words are:

1. Root Chakra = Red; Earth; Understanding and Acceptance.
2. Sacral Chakra = Orange; Water; Creativity and Sensitivity.
3. Solar Plexus Chakra = Yellow; Fire; Commitment.
4. Heart Chakra = Green; Air; Divine Love and Compassion.
5. Throat Chakra = Blue; Sound; Truth and Expression.
6. Third Eye Chakra = Indigo; Light: Intuition, Vision and Hearing.
7. Crown Chakra = Violet; Thought; Boundlessness, Thought and Will.

If you are ill or become ill, take action and be a participant in creating your own health. Read, learn, and research. Do not leave your life solely in the hands of others, including me. As there is a wealth of information available about the nature and functioning of chakras, only a surface perspective will be given here as it relates most succinctly to so-called HIV+ symptoms and general disease in the body. I assure you that as you learn of the chakras, you will more than likely be drawn to learn further on your own. A reader need only have basic knowledge to begin to change thinking patterns, speak perfect health, seek the (g)od within and restore total well-being. There must be a complete willingness to let go of *Momma's God*, a metaphor for accepting what others teach you, rather than allowing your consciousness to unfold. The real gift of divinity is within you, as you.

Remember, good teaching does not put anything inside of you. It merely draws out what is already there. We are all students of life. Believing defines realities, while experiencing dissolves realities. What you "believe" is immensely different from what you "know." What you believe is usually what others tell you. What you "know" is a different matter. It just is! It is true for you because you experienced it directly. While there are many truths, you can relax knowing that your truth is your own. You can see, feel and experience the fruits of it.

The Path to Wholeness and Healing

The main purpose in working with and understanding the chakras is to create integration and wholeness within yourself. You can come to know and accept the different aspects of yourself (physical, material, sexual, spiritual, etc.), which work together to help you gain tremendous insight into how you, through your thinking, speaking and feeling affect your body, mind and circumstances in life. The awareness attained gives you the advantage of being able to make choices and decisions from a place of balance, rather than being blindly influenced by forces you do not understand. You learn to give the gift of love to yourself and to all of creation. Love is the source of all healing.

During meditation which is discussed later, energy is focused on the following principles, each of which corresponds to a chakra in your body, from root to crown. The Principles of The Chakras are:

1. All Is One.
2. Honor One Another.
3. Respect Yourself.

4. Love Is Divine Power.
5. Surrender Personal Will To Divine Will.
6. Seek Only The Truth.
7. Live In The Present Moment.

Optimally functioning chakras will carry you from embodiment to enlightenment. From the lower three chakras where reside earthly material pleasures and your inner world and personal reality, you can ascend through the heart of unconditional love and compassion to the higher chakras of universal reality, where you focus on communication, insight and wholeness. The realization of a transformation from darkness to light towards (g)od-realization can occur.

If you observe yourself or another exhibiting any of the following behaviors (also listen in chapter one), be aware that bodily illnesses serve as red flags to alert you to the related chakra energy imbalances: insecurity, arrogance, conceit, vanity, aloofness, anger and rage, jealousy, possessiveness, blaming others, self-doubt, constantly giving in to those in authority, resisting change, laziness, impatience, excessive worrying, over-sensitivity to the opinions of others, intense erotic fantasies, feelings of being misunderstood, shame, excessive need for sympathy and other less desirable behaviors. Again, you create your existence by your thinking and emotions.

On the other hand, the following behaviors inevitably yield a free-functioning, free-flowing, energy-balanced root chakra: down to earth and grounded personality, courage, comfort in the physical body, generosity, empathy, compassion, confidence, sensitivity, ability to cry easily, creativity, warrior-like nature, power, faithfulness in the divine, selfless to service to others, spontaneity, and the ability to let go into "being-ness," instead of "doing-ness."

Thinking patterns and behaviors invariably affect energy moving through the chakras. Thoughts are great, living, dynamic things that have force in the universe. When you entertain healthy thoughts, you keep good health. Without a doubt, when you hold on to thoughts of diseased tissues, weak nerves, thoughts of improper functioning of organs or viscera, you can never expect good health, beauty or harmony within yourself. "As a man thinks in his heart, so is he." "Man is created by thought. What a man thinks upon, that he becomes."

> *I want to interject something very important here specifically to my homosexual brothers who are under attack and who often seem to have a difficult time with these concepts. I said this before, but let me say it again: "Be what you is and not what you ain't, 'cause if you ain't what you is, then you is what you ain't." As a same gender loving, homosexual man, you as any other person have the choice and the ability to transcend your lower basic animal urges in deference to higher spiritual powers. Know also that you must give to others that which you wish to receive. There is not a way in the world to feel better about self by putting down another person. If your personality, sense of humor and sense of self is such that you are one who thinks it funny to constantly berate and/or find fault in others, then let go of that aspect of your personality—for your own good and your own good health.*

Start giving thanks right now, this very instant for all that you are. Be thankful for your illness. Embrace your wonderful self as you are. Give yourself over to the goodness that you are. See yourself as one with all that is, even those you think you hate or who hate you. You are an integral part of the universe. God loves you. I love you. You love you. You know you do. Do not let anyone tell you otherwise. No words in any book can negate what you know in your heart of hearts. You are the way you are because it is as it should be unless you choose to be otherwise. You are truly a blessing to the world.

Always remember those who came before you. Remember the homosexuals who made contributions to humanity. There was only one James Baldwin and there will never be another. He reminded you *"The most dangerous creation of any society is the man who has nothing to lose."* Remind yourself of *The Color of Purple* author and poet, Alice Walker, who said, *"What the mind doesn't understand, it worships or fears."* Take pride in the fact that the Civil Rights March creator, Baynard Rustin, was a homosexual who was pushed into the background but whose contributions can never be denied. Be a warrior. Remember, it was Mr. Rustin who said, *"When the individual is protesting society's refusal to acknowledge his dignity, his very protest confers dignity on him."* Democratic dynamo Barbara Jordan, said, *"All Blacks are militant in their gifts, but militancy is expressed in different ways."* Acclaimed author Lorraine Hansberry wrote, *"The thing that makes you exceptional, if you are at all, is the very thing that must make you lonely."* Johnny Mathis was simply, *"Wonderful"*.

Go ahead and smile. Rejoice, because it rings true in your body that you are divine. Your healing is already here. It is already all right."

Energy travels from the spiritual realm, affects the mind, and eventually crystallizes in the physical body. Come to understand natural and sacred laws that govern your body. Returning to the chakras, you can come to understand all of life's experiences. You are encouraged not to take for granted what is written here but to experience it for yourself, for experience is the highest teacher. Allow health to be restored to your body.

While healing is a gift and already exists in you in the present moment, it must be made manifest in your body. Health exists inside you and is waiting to flourish. Having basic knowledge of the significance and function of each chakra can clear blockages through effort and meditation. That is what is taught in this book.

Know that effort must be applied to learn and gain understanding of the chakras and the state of "feeling meditation." Daily practice must be applied. Just as one would practice playing a musical instrument to acquire skill, practice is required to access the energy of the chakras and clear any blockages. Remember, blockages result from ill-thinking generated from years of conditioning thrust upon you by other humans who claim the existence of HIV.

It may be difficult for those you who are learning a new and different way of thinking and being, but it will become easier when you become as a child, and allow the information presented here to seep into your consciousness. Prepare yourself for a moving experience full of wonderment and physical sensation. I have found no experience that brings me more joy than the feeling of divine energy coursing throughout my body, miraculously realigning the universe within. It literally brings tears of joy to my eyes to feel so connected to my own body while experiencing the flow of divine love in action throughout my being.

Again, a note of caution to the reader not only to come to understand the information presented, but to use daily meditation in order to "feel into it." Feeling must be practiced, for understanding without feeling leads to dis-ease. Feel without reaching. Passively allow what is happening in your mind and body to speak to you. In fact, whenever there is a load of information incorporated into your body, there must also be movement of the emotions to ensure balance of your body system. Otherwise, illnesses can occur. There can be what is considered to be "too much consciousness." Ergo, the emotions must be allowed to catch up, so to speak.

Do not use intoxicating or mind-altering substances to gain temporary relief from consciousness phenomenon. You are called to surrender addictions, even addiction to sex. Addictive behavior sometimes signifies an attempt to slow down an overbearing consciousness by letting the emotions slip out of control. A false sense of balance between forces in the body may be experienced for a short while emotions are expressed, ventilated or unloaded. Drunkenness might signify that you are overwhelmed with divinity. Imagine that. Television, a job, sex, food, relationships, socializing, the internet, drugs etc. can all become addictive. Aside from helping you gain temporary relief from "too much consciousness," addictions might also be a means of escape, when you refuse to face feelings arising from your subconscious mind. Expanded consciousness must be balanced with emotional movement, or there is a danger of creating illness in your body.

Chant for Self-Esteem

Earth, Water, Fire, and Air
Within me all things are there.

Flesh on my bones is life the earth.
It's soft but strong and full of worth.

The Blood that flows between my veins
Is like the ocean, river and rain.

My spirit soars and takes me higher.
Here is where I keep my fire.

My breath and thoughts are like the air.
I can do anything and go everywhere.

Earth, Water, Fire and Air
Within me all things are there.

And so I pledge unto myself
Power, Love, Health, and Wealth.

--Luisah Teish, Jumbalaya

The Elements of Earth, Water, Fire and Air

The elements around us are often more familiar to many people
than the chakras of the body. Did you know that the four physical
elements are inextricably related to four of your chakras? *Earth*
represents your foundation, substance, abundance and connection to
your family and your life purpose. It is linked to your root chakra.
Water is indicative of your emotional nature and ability to release such:
healing, inner reflection, intuition, self-regard and self-exploration, as
well as unconditional love. Water is associated with your sacral chakra.
Fire provides the energy to propel self-transformation by sometimes
revealing your vulnerabilities. Through courage and faith in your own
power to rebel when necessary and live your truth and life purpose, you
learn to balance the physical, emotional and mental aspects of yourself.
This powerful element is related to your solar plexus chakra. A*ir*, with
its ability to change directions, represents your mind, or the intellect,
and your connection to the Creator. It is linked to your heart chakra.
With its compassion, you can change from being closed-minded to
being an open-minded individual. The remaining three chakras, the
throat, third eye and crown chakras, also known as the *Heaven chakras*
also have "elemental" associations. They are sound, light and thought,
respectively.

These relationships will also show up in the more detailed following
sections. They will help you understand and embrace the concepts
explained there.

Red, Root Chakra, All Is One

The root chakra positioned between the genitals and the anus represents our connection to *Mother Earth* and Her magnetic essence. From the root chakra stems the foundation for all life. Its main function is "embodiment," and signals our arrival into the physical vehicle to experience life, whose wonderful and sometimes difficult situations present us with the opportunity to either accept our reality, or to change it.

The energy of the root chakra has the effect of grounding life in the physical plane of existence. Consequently, the base of the spine, legs, bones, feet rectum and immune system are affected by root chakra functioning.

Optimally healthy people are comfortable in their own skin, and like their body as it is, because they feel themselves connected to others and the earth. They are less likely to be fearful of change, or rigid, as well as other less positive qualities that are preferable in people. They are full of energy and able to let go and remain stable and practical, while exhibiting qualities as being generous, loyal and down to earth.

Yet, these qualities are not overly exhibited. The root chakra has earth as its element, stability, solidity, unity and form are key words used when describing it.

Perception of the physical world, motivation, will, and intent is governed here. Physical dysfunction of this chakra, include chronic lower back pain, sciatica, varicose veins, rectal tumors and cancer, depression and immune related disorders. Certain eye, ear and throat disorders are also indicative of disturbances in root chakra energies.

So-called HIV+ symptoms can be seen primarily as root chakra disturbances. Many who show symptoms have become isolated from friends and lovers, families and society in general. While a person by all outside appearances presents him/herself as normal and well adjusted, within the person are feelings of alienation and non-acceptance by the very core people who represent love and security in their life.

Some homosexual people who are diagnosed so-called HIV+ are disowned by their friends and family, and are sometimes left to live without the comfort and closeness of others. Whether this has actually happened or not, a person in this situation could feel (emotionally) that s/he has lost grounding to all that provides safety and security in an otherwise hostile world. A fearful person can be easily affected by continued reports of the HIV crisis and suggestions of who is most likely to contract the disease. This can result in an inner chaos that sets the stage for illness to prevail. Personal integrity wanes and there is a diminution of will to love and respect self. Again, where the mind goes, the body will follow. An otherwise confident, secure person can become a victim of the power of suggestion. His/her mind can come under the control of another. S/he can begin to hate the skin /she is in, feel defenseless against the world and literally worry himself/herself to death because s/he has come to believe that because his/her behavior has been deemed inappropriate, s/he is worthy of death. On a subtler level, s/he believes that, because of sex and sexuality issues s/he is not accepted for being the person s/he is.

Clearing blockages through meditation in the root chakra restores vitality to the physical body, unleashes the life force within and allows one to create courage, stability and health. It is a process of releasing tension along the spine by letting go of fear and insecurity, self-centeredness, anger, greed and violence.

You can literally know a person by their illnesses. "Any problem you have, whether it is a physical ailment, negative emotion(s), faulty beliefs or rigid dogmatic spiritual perceptions, stems from or creates stuck energy. To completely heal from an ailment you must release the stagnant energy that is at the underlying cause.

Individuals, societies and whole nations are being overcome with HIV symptoms due to deficiencies and/or blockages in chakra energies brought on by fear and promulgated by media and the medical profession—many of whom are unaware of the detrimental actions of their mislead passions. Moreover, over-exposure to toxic drugs damages the body and sometimes results in death.

These statements make strong assertions, but are in no way in intended to deny advances made in medicine that are providing help and hope to those who believe themselves ill. The universe responds to each person where s/he is in consciousness development. Further, all perspective emanates from Spirit. You are spirit manifested in physical form. I am merely contending here that there is more to the maintenance of health than meets the eye of the microscope. Expand your awareness from the physical to the spiritual. You are a spiritual being having a physical experience on earth.

Make it your goal to free yourself from certain "group contagion" and from negative "group think" that precludes your ability to think for yourself about your own health and wellness. Train your thoughts on self-love and acceptance, perfect health, and your ability to transcend any apparent difficulty in life. Gaining an understanding of the root chakra is essential in creating a firm base from which to make an ascent through the chakras having learned divine unity.

Use the resources in Appendix (A), as well as the *Rainbow Warrior Companion* that comes with this book, and visit my website www.consciousdr.com to study the facts of research about why the prevailing paradigm about HIV is questionable, at best, a hoax. I say, there is no HIV. Learn to take your own health into your own hands.

Orange, Sacral Chakra,
Honor One Another.

The sacral chakra, positioned in the sacrum and lower abdomen of the lower vertebrae, is the "sacred" dwelling place of the *Self*, which functions to let us know our true inner beauty and strength. Self-worth and self-love grows as the individual-self and the self-as-divine-spirit is fused. Just as the name implies, there must be the recognition that, *"Who I Am Is Divine."* There must also be a sacred purpose to life. In becoming aware of your sacred purpose you are guided by your soul, which knows the exact path you are to take in this life. By experiencing pain, illness, relationship troubles, and many other perceived adverse life experiences, you then question your existence and your purpose in life. In this way, the sacral chakra houses your inner knowing of who you are.

The organs of the body impacted by the energy of the sacral chakra are the sexual organs, large intestine, lower vertebrae, pelvis, appendix, bladder, and hip area. Those with fewer disruptions in energy flow through this chakra are less likely to be overly blaming of others for difficulties in their own lives. They are more likely to release feelings of guilt when perhaps making perceived mistakes in life. Energy flows freely when you refuse to allow money worries and power and control issues to hamper your creativity, individual beauty, wisdom and love of self.

Ethics in relationships are likely to be observed, as well. Hence, physical dysfunction as sexual potency, pelvic and low back pain, urinary problems, venereal disease and sciatica are prevalent in those who have an energy blockage in this chakra. There would also likely be a loss of identity, low self-worth and less respect for self.

The element of *water* is indicative of the sacral chakra, which cleanses and has a centering quality, ebbing and flowing, creating mood changes in the person. It is essential for a person to allow all emotion to be felt but balanced. Damned up feelings as well as over-expression of emotion would prevent sacral energy flow.

Develop the increased inclination to listen to your body. The sacral chakra, housing the sexual and reproductive organs holds that sex can be a sacred and divine act that has the ability to draw energy out from the center of your being into the universal force field. Your energy is replenished, and returns to the core center when orgasm is experienced. The physical body and mind completely let go and surrender to your soul and spirit. The resulting period of spontaneous relaxation has a cleansing effect on your body.

Many often try to portray sex as a dirty act when in fact sex is probably one of the most healing experiences you can have. What better way to reduce stress than with loving touches and sensual caresses? Even still, many religions and cultures have insisted on establishing sexual rules or barriers between human beings that label sex outside of these human-conceived conditions as bad, dirty or sinful. They tell you that homosexual union is immoral and therefore deserving of punishment.

When a homosexual person refuses to adopt the position that sex out of wedlock is inappropriate, or that gay people are abominations, s/he is in a much better position to maintain health. Refuse to allow culture and society to label you abnormal. By developing a personal relationship with the divine spirit within, you will find the greatest love of self, imaginable; one that goes beyond deed. It is a love that just is. You are a child of *The Most High God*. When you recognize that love within you, you can then see beauty in all its wondrous forms, yourself in particular. You can then begin to see yourself in everyone you meet. You can also accept and appreciate the heart and soul of those different from you.

Sexuality that is unencumbered by guilt and shame has the power to stimulate spirituality and refresh and rebalance the entire mind/body system. The act of sex is only impure when it is practiced for egoistic or malicious reasons, or to hurt others. Remember the principle of the sacral chakra is to "honor one another" in every way.

A person with physical symptoms of illness must recognize beauty irrespective of what others say or believe. It is no wonder that gay men are not the only people unconsciously self-inflicting so-called HIV symptoms on themselves (symptoms related to guilt, shame, anger, rejection, etc.) while blaming others for giving them the disease. The HIV crisis is branching out from the homosexual community and is now being experienced by people from all walks of life. Homosexual, straight, bisexual, and adults and teenage people from all races and socioeconomic strata are now being targeted for HIV testing.

Fear of contracting illness is eating away at our societies and the world by killing citizens and lining the pockets of pharmaceutical companies *(Big Pharma)*, healthcare and other industries. Count the number of pharmaceutical commercials you see in the course of your tell-lie-vision viewing, not to mention during major tell-lie-vision news programs. We are almost constantly bombarded with fear, lies and deception.

You might be amazed to learn that according to an article posted at *The Huffington Post* website, pharmaceutical companies spend more money advertising their drugs than they do researching them (Eichler, 2013).

Consider that children and teens are bombarded with sexual images through all forms of media, while at the same time being asked to remain abstinent until marriage. They are excited by their bodies' awakening, but are terrified and ashamed to experience the gift of sexual expression. These statements are not meant to advocate or promote teenage sexual activity, but to point out that age does make a difference in a person's ability to think abstractly and to psychologically defend against the onslaught of confusion, hate and fear surrounding sex and sexuality. If a teen decides to become sexually active, s/he should not be intimidated or threatened into feelings of shame and worthlessness. Mixed messages and circular reasoning can lead to regret and worry, which have a way of breaking down even the healthiest of people. The body is swift to respond to fear.

Negative, harmful e-motions (energy in motion) all stem from the inability to take in life with a sense of joy and hope for the future. In turn, they set the stage for disease. What follows is loss of respect and love for self when we feel guilty and ashamed about our sexuality, and our divine right to be as we are.

Understanding of the sacral chakra can help you realign the energy of this energy center, and foster health in your body, mind and spirit, by helping facilitate the recognition of beauty in life, in every sense of the word. In fact, begin to see it all around you: in nature, in others and even in those who wrong you. The lessons of the sacral chakra teach you to do all of this, as well as to enjoy being in the company of others both like you and different from you. Express love and know friendship. Here, again, love is the key. Love's divine expression alone conquers fear, the enemy. Energy must flow freely through the sacral chakra to restore health to a dis-eased body.

By expanding and liberating all of life's aspects, including sexual energy, you can raise awareness of the world within and around, in every moment of waking-life. You can also develop your unique self as a universal being, leaving you feeling at home in the *"Self."* Then, praise others and stop all criticism. Stop scaring yourself with your thoughts and begin to be gentle, kind, and patient with others and yourself. You can then look into the mirror and say, "I love you." You can look at others and say, "I love you", and mean it.

Again, the principle of the sacral chakra is to "Honor One Another."

Take a moment here to again give thanks to the Creator for your illness if you perceive that you have one. You are returning to the awareness that you are loved utterly. You are being shown the way back to the fullness of joy in spirit. Full health is now restored. The way you look at life will never be the same. You are aware that you are the power. You overcome when you honor divine others.

Use your most powerful sexual healing energy responsibly, with love.

When unity has been grounded in the root chakra and the consciousness that all is one is lived, you can then ascend to the sacral chakra. You can allow your sexual desire and sexual energies to stimulate confidence, creativity, intimacy and the desire to enhance your relationships, not by domination but through balance and love. You learn to honor others in everything you do. Doing so, allows you to ascend the chakra column, heal and become divine.

Yellow, Solar Plexus Chakra,
Respect Yourself

As we continue our journey through the chakras we increase our soul consciousness, entering the place of power deep within. We recognized that at the root chakra we forge stability and courage by understanding and appreciating our innate gifts we brought with us into the world. In the sacral chakra, we gained confidence in ourselves with self-knowledge, and accepted our creative selves by honoring all others. Now you are ready to examine your relationship with yourself.

Before reading this section, take an additional moment to do a bit of introspection. Acknowledge that if you experienced the trauma of hearing that you were so-called HIV+, the recent years of your life and perhaps many years of living in fear of one day becoming HIV+ have been ruled by fear. Pain, frustration, anger and despair have taken over your life. Joy of living has been depleted. All of your relationships with others have been based on issues of fear, inhibiting you from moving forward in life, preventing you from forgiving others, and thus attempting to control them. And indeed, yes, you have been unable to forgive yourself. Rather than being in control of your emotions, you have become controlled by your emotions. Upon acknowledging this fact, you are ready to move forward in your learning and upward through the chakras toward true self-realization. Further, you are ready to accept that your body has volunteered to show you that you need to release old hurts, forgive yourself for perceived mistakes, and love yourself unconditionally.

The solar plexus chakra is positioned in the solar plexus area and has yellow as its color. This chakra is all about *will*, personal power and taking action. When you have a balanced solar plexus chakra, you use your ego for enthusiasm, drive and success, and you demonstrate healthy self-esteem and self-respect. Your solar plexus chakra governs your stomach, intestines, liver, bladder, spleen and skin. Imbalance in this area leads to ulcers, diabetes, liver and pancreas malfunction, and exhibits your need for power over others, especially when you are in a consciousness of fear, indifference and self-loathing. Those who think themselves infected with so-called HIV are prone to manifesting physical symptoms that they are at "dis-ease with self" when they allow others to take their power or when they themselves attempt to drain others' energies. However, assessing the energy of the chakras through meditation restores optimal functioning through the solar plexus area of your body.

The element of fire is associated with the solar plexus chakra. Transform rage into radiance by understanding its fiery energy. Located below the breastbone at the base of the sternum, the solar plexus chakra is your fear center and the center of personal power. There, the expression of creativity is enhanced through the balance of that power. Just below the navel and above the waist, the solar plexus chakra vitalizes your digestive processes, metabolism and your emotions. The pancreas, muscles, nervous system, liver, gall bladder and adrenals are all affected by solar plexus functioning. Consequently, when blockages in this chakra occur due to fear, physical dysfunction including indigestion, gastric ulcers, hepatitis, liver dysfunction and diarrhea can manifest. Problems such as arthritis, anorexia, and bulimia can persist when you fail to realize that all of life's experiences, particularly the painful ones, have the potential to prod you forward into a better understanding of yourself and others.

The fear associated with this chakra, when transcended with love, is invaluable to self-development. People tend to fear being powerful as much as they fear being powerless. Holding on to pain by not forgiving others only holds you back, not the other person. An unforgiving spirit keeps you from crossing the bridge to self-love.

The fiery energy of the solar plexus chakra also teaches you to assert your personal power by refusing to allow others to mistake your kindness for weakness. Place what you were taught about turning the other cheek in proper perspective. You are a **g-o-d** in the making, a (**G**enerator-**O**perator-**D**estroyer). Like Sekhmet, you sometimes have to love yourself enough to destroy that which is attempting to destroy you. Sometimes you have to fight fire with fire.

When you are unable to move your own life forward you tend to draw needy others into your world. They ask you for money you do not have, for more than enough of your time and attention or for any number of ill-suited requests and demands that are likely upset you. Be mindful or aware of what is taking place by listening to your body.

If you experience stomach pain, ulcers, kidney problems or indigestion, examine issues of anger and fear in your life as they pertain to self and others. You may find that your head is telling you one thing but your gut is telling you another. Find the strength to stand your ground with those who appear to be taking advantage of you. Remember, that you drew the person into your life in order that you might learn to love, honor and respect yourself. Speak your piece (peace) respectfully, follow it up with action, and experience the wonders of the universe within.

Bodily illness can be viewed as an expression of divine grace. The cells of your body are working together to provide a vessel for your soul's growth. Illness has a way of guiding you into understanding your own personal growth. Have you learned to forgive yourself and others? Have you learned to be thankful in both perceived good times and bad times? Be honest with yourself.

Determine your relationship to others in your life. Do you find upon contemplation that most of your behavior towards others is governed by what you can get from them? Are you nice to others so that you can receive something from them? Are you a selfish person? Do you lack confidence when not around familiar others? Are you loud and aggressive? Do you find yourself unkind and uncaring when things don't go your way? Do you notice that you are frequently unaware of your own or other people's feelings? Do your emotions flare up easily? Are you likely to resort to violence when unable to resolve conflicts with others?

If you answered yes to any one of these questions, you are living a life relating to others out of fear rather than love. Perhaps without even realizing it, you are giving your power away to others who you think you are controlling.

Now is the time to regain a life of laughter, joy and passion. You will now learn to express felt emotions with ease. While you may feel sadness, you will not allow it to become despair. You might experience conflict, anger and rage, yet you will not allow yourself to become violent. Many people are realizing that there is a correlation between people who have beliefs in violence and the likelihood and proneness to having accidents.

When life succumbs to being ruled by fear, the stage for dis-ease and illness is set. Fear hampers growth. Love expands growth. Fear creates illness. Love creates health.

Are you aware that when you degrade others or simply see something in them that you do not like, you are projecting onto them what you do not like about yourself? In other words, what you do not like in other people can be reflective of what you do not like in yourself. In fact, you would not even recognize it in them if you did not see the potential for that very same thing in yourself.

The moment you come to realize and accept this, you can immediately vow to become one with every person that exists in the world. Being non-judgmental of others helps to lift the burden of fear that binds our love for all that is.

Know that whether you perceive an experience to be good or bad, it was you who drew the experience to yourself as a lesson. It is your thinking about how you relate to the world that determines the outcome. In this light, when you perceive that an impending situation is negative, you block the flow of (love) energy. However, when you are able to see yourself in every person you meet, you open the flow for love. Those whom you perceive as bringing you bad news have done only one thing in your life: they have moved you forward from where you were in your own thinking. When you realize this, you have then successfully made perceptual adjustments which can advise your health.

When you begin to heal the dark parts of your own personality, you refocus energy away from your ego back to consciousness awareness of self-love and self-respect. Recognizing this type thinking each time it arises and acknowledging your oneness with others provides a way to generate love for others while re-energizing yourself and clearing the way for the flow of divine love. Dis-ease with self and disease in the body, in this case, is derailed and health is maintained.

Release from consciousness old patterns of thinking and behavior, and yield to the flow of the rhythms of life, being mindful to respect and love yourself. It was Nelson Mandela who reiterated what Marianne Williamson shared that; *"Our deepest fear is not that we are inadequate. Our deepest fear is that we are powerful beyond measure."* Loving treatment of self and others heals you and others.

How, then are you to overcome the seemingly difficult task of redirecting your energies away from your ego? Bear in mind that the ego sometimes knows only its selfish desires. It might prod you into believing that it is conceivable to gain personal power by degrading others. How are you to harness personal power without thinking yourself better than others? It is advantageous for you to begin to see the beauty of universal design which is an intricate cosmic web of happenstance that draws beneficial events into your life which provide guidance toward the realization that you are one with *"All That Is."*

First, you must ask your higher self that it be done. *"Seek and You Shall Find."* Know that whatever you ask shall be given to you. You are the creator of it. Your intentions will lead you to reach the goals you desire. You have then, in word and thought, spoken that which you desire into existence.

As sure as the sun will rise and set on the morrow, your being will be led to the realization that all things exist for the good of those who know and demonstrate the power of love. It is through others that you gain knowledge and "over"-standing of yourself. That person or situation exists so that you might learn and grow in the glory of your higher self. Coming in contact with that person or situation is merely a projection of your own inner world. Whatever is in your mind has drawn a lesson that has the potential of leading you into better knowing, understanding and love of yourself, for what you give to another, you give to yourself. Until the lesson is learned, similar experiences will be presented to you again and again. You are familiar with the adage that, "what goes around comes around." So treat people like you want them to treat you, with unconditional love.

Through the act of selfless service, you begin to move away from ego-centeredness which creates tremendous disharmony in the world, toward consciously working for the good of all people and the environment. It is an acceptance of the fact that all perfect gifts given are from the creator of all that is. It is not from your own pockets that the gift is given but from the fullness and abundance of the universe that you receive and pass those blessings on to others. You can and should do this mentally as well. You have been given everything that you have, and you are to share your gifts and talents with others. Any thought of lack or limitation in your life cuts you off from inheriting both material and spiritual wealth.

Everything in your existence is a result of your consciousness. Seek to be your higher self, and live as if you are in full awareness of your higher self. In fact, there is not a place you can go without it.

Anything that is not all good is "no-thing" at all. It is a lie. It in fact is not real. Begin to characterize these illusions as such. They appear real but are "no-thing."

Receiving an HIV+ diagnosis has the potential to teach self-love to those who think themselves less than completely loved. Any person suffering from physical symptoms of dis-ease with self has believed otherwise. Perhaps without even realizing it, s/he has is closing the portals of divine energy which courses throughout the body and sustains the physical form.

Homosexual men in particular should remember that they are "gatekeepers." Same-Gender- Loving (SGL) men and women guard the doors between the physical and spiritual world. Without them, the earth would be unable to balance its energies. It would collapse unto itself. As stated by Malidoma Patrice Some, West African writer/healer of the Dagara tribe and author of *Of Water and the Spirit*, *"You are the gatekeepers, shamans and healers of the tribe, the global tribe."* Love yourself and others.

Examine the roots of fear, for it is fear that can obstruct the stream of divine love waiting to emanate from your innermost place of being. Fear manifests as false expectations that appear real. Fear can cause your stomach to rumble. Listen to your body as it guides you from embodiment of the lower three chakras towards enlightenment of the upper chakras. Fear can stifle spiritual growth and challenge your desire to operate from a position of love. It is fear that can inflame your body and speed dis-ease. It is fear that can keep you from being all that you are until you move in more productive ways.

Fear plays an integral and necessary part in development during your life. The mere recognition of it can trigger you to observe your own thoughts, words and actions in that very moment.

You may discover that you unconsciously choose fear, in order to grow. Fear has a way of spurring you on to right decision-making. By this, I mean that you may create life experiences that result in dire consequences. Yet even in the midst of the pain, you learn about yourself. Regardless of the situation, you will find that when you boldly examine your fears and refuse to run away while infusing them with divine love, they dissolve. What you resist, persists. Never forget that you are the light of the world. You can create out of an entirely different mode of thinking and being; the mode of love for all that is, the mode of love and respect for yourself, no matter what. Acknowledge that you are pure love, power, strength, creativity, peace and health.

Feel the gift you have given yourself. Now, smile! Perhaps there are even tears of joy when you respect your divine self.

You can research the HIV debacle and crisis for yourself and reach your own informed decision about how to heal yourself. There is not better form of self-respect. Again, see and study your Rainbow Companion at <u>www.consciousdr.com</u>. There are videos there for your viewing which can also be shared with others. You will be astounded at just how much scientific information has been kept hidden from you by mass media and corporate medical doctors.

Green, Heart Chakra,
Love Is Divine Power

The heart chakra is positioned in the center of the thoracic cavity and is associated with the color green and the element of air. When this chakra is functioning optimally, we are able to love and be loved and exhibit unconditional positive regard, acceptance and peace with others. When this chakra is not in alignment, lung and breathing problems, upper back pain, blood diseases, and breast cancer can result. A person traumatized and ostracized by an HIV+ diagnosis, though mainly a root chakra disturbance, can also experience heart chakra illnesses.

The heart chakra is the crossroads between transformation and spiritual life. It actually stands midway between physical life and spiritual life. Heart chakra lessons present the challenge of gaining insights into the nature of suffering, quelling confusion and restoring hopefulness and trust in God. It teaches us to love our enemy. It teaches that suffering brings understanding. From a position of understanding great love is possible. Love is universal. The "heart of love" is beyond words or description. It just is.

This is the birth of understanding; understanding that our enemy suffers as we do. Begin to see through the eyes of compassion, for without compassion there can be no love. Without love, there can be no physical, mental or emotional health. When there is a lack of love, there is confusion and frustration. Confusion and frustration keep you from recognizing your "soul purpose" and inhibit your ascent through the chakras into the universal realms towards enlightenment. We are all one people and must learn to love universally.

As life is a continual cycle of birth, growth and return, I found that at the moment of writing this section I was struggling with heart chakra lessons. I pondered how could I possibly heal the wounds of the world when I seemingly couldn't heal my own? I was unable to write for weeks.

Negative thinking, I now know, kept me from manifesting the desires of my heart. I could not go forward in life while unresolvedly looking back. I prayed earnestly throughout the day for guidance. I needed to accept my divine right to change my mind about what it is that I wanted to do with my life, where I wanted to work and what I was willing to tolerate as part of it. Each time I experienced feelings of remorse about voluntarily resigning from my job I changed my thinking to the remembering of all the good times and the times when seeming bad experiences led to higher understanding. In order to move forward to another phase of life, I released the judgment against myself that the decision I made was a wrong one. I loved while there and would love with truth and compassion wherever I decided to go.

Heart chakra lessons are directly related to lessons of forgiveness of others and self, compassion, understanding, balance, group consciousness, oneness in life, acceptance, peace, openness, harmony and contentment. If you choose not to address these life issues you will continue to be out of balance and experience emotional instability. I felt as if I had put myself through the ringer, feeling as if I could not move forward in life because I made wrong decisions in my recent life. I wallowed in self-pity. Consequently, I was not able to fully devote myself to potential new opportunities. I worried incessantly about financial insecurities, became possessive of money, refused to give more to charities and homeless people or needful friends. Mistrustful of others' intentions, I blamed others for my own challenges in life. I doubted my self-worth and my ability to create a rich and abundant life for myself. I had become almost totally thwarted. I had temporarily become a recluse. I used that time to reorganize my thoughts about which direction I wanted to go in my life

Why did I feel ashamed about decisions I made in life? Why was I compelled to hold on to the past? Could it be that I was using past relationships to predict what would happen in the future? Was I keeping my fears alive by holding to my attachment to the past and perhaps even the future? I was definitely unable to fully enjoy living in the present. Why was I unable to feel that I deserved to have healthy relationships? Was I thinking that I could somehow control the future? Would this somehow give me the illusion of being safe?

Admittedly, I was fearful that the past would repeat itself and that I would develop unsuccessful relationships. Just as I had come to realize that no one gave me so-called HIV, I came to realize that no one could make me happy or make my relationships successful but me. I could not change other people. I could only change my relation or adaptation to them. I could no longer blame others for my own happiness and peace of mind.

I learned to release feelings of guilt as well as those of blame. I could no longer play the victim. Nor could I continue to punish myself for past decisions. Only then could I move forward into new relationships and live fully in the present. I realized that I was getting off the track of helplessness and onto the road to self-empowerment. My only limitations would be the ones I placed on myself.

I prayed to be better able to be aware the thoughts and feelings that came to my mind: thoughts of limitation and lack, issues of power and control, and concerns with authority figures. I had to learn to see the world as a friendly place, see the planet as loving and see others' perceived negative behaviors as denied parts of myself that needed to be healed. I had to see the storms of life as a necessity for spiritual growth. I gave heart-felt thanks to the Creator of All for all magnificent blessings of synchronicity. As Rocco Errico said in his book *And Then There Was Light*, it was as if the storm had come and God said to me, "I AM coming to you in a cloud." Thunder had given power and light to my revelations and lightening illumined my intuition.

I had to allow others to love me and be concerned about me and about my future. My selfish paranoia kept me from accepting love and concern from my friends. I felt deep within my being that friends were only concerned about me inasmuch as they wanted to experience joy in my failure. This I know was a serious problem that I had within me. Feelings of unworthiness crept into my consciousness when I felt vulnerable and my mind was deluged with negative thoughts, self-loathing and fear.

Suddenly, I remembered, *"Abide in me. Keep the faith in my word and I will bring it to pass. Whatsoever you ask when you pray shall be given unto you."* It would swiftly come to pass; whatever I needed. If I was healed from so-called HIV, I would certainly be relieved of ill thinking. I began to give praise and the gates of love opened, alleviating stress, restoring health in my body, leaving no room for thoughts of self-criticism. My heart began to feel lighter. My lungs expanded and contracted. My shoulders and arms, ribs and chest, diaphragm and thymus received a surge of energy, lifted my spirit and harmonized my body, and left me at peace with the process of life.

When friends who had been ill, died from so-called HIV complications and toxic drugs, I felt profound sadness. I wanted to somehow do something to help change people's perspective about HIV. I wanted to reach out to the world, but not as part of any organization such as *AID Atlanta/Evolution Project* or *Project Open Hand*, organizations I felt operated from a perspective of fear of contracting a disease I knew did not exist; organizations funded by a government I was not sure I could trust.

~ What were their agendas?
~ Why had I seen so many advertisements that seemed to target gay, Black men and women?
~ Why had I never heard country radio stations urge people to go to the nearest mall and have their mouth swabbed to find out "their status"? Why had I only heard those advertisements on Black radio stations?
~ Why had nearly every homosexual magazine or newspaper publication I viewed have homosexual, Black men on every 5th page who were urged to "know your status"? Where were the advertisements for White and Asian, and Hispanic guys urging them to know their status?
~ Were Black homosexuals being portrayed as promiscuous and overly sexualized?
~ Were Black people's sexual practices somehow different from other races of people?
~ Why were the prescribed toxic drugs being marketed to Black homosexuals in almost every advertisement I saw?

I had learned from direct experience, that ingesting highly-toxic, prescribed HIV drugs (Epivir and Zerit) resulted in numbness in my finger and toes, *Peripheral Neuropathy* (PN). I had already learned the **direct-effects**, not so-called side-effects. I had seen friends and associates whose breasts became enlarged *(Gynecomastia)* after ingesting the drugs for long periods of time. I had seen that others who took the drugs for an extended period were wearing *leg-pumps* to increase blood circulation in their arms and hands, legs and feet. How sad it was to see their nervous system was so damaged from ARVs that they experienced *irregular gait*. How sad it was to see a once healthy person, hobble down the street thinking that taking the ARV drugs they are taking are what is saving their life.

I questioned everything. Why did ARVs block the synthesis of DNA at the mitochondrial level, the powerhouse of the cell? What was happening around me made no sense. Why was everybody I knew who had been told that they were HIV+ getting sick(er) after taking the drugs? Many of them had no symptoms of physical illness when they took the HIV antibody test. Many of the ones who trusted their doctors, died.

There was so much hysteria that seemingly nobody but me was analyzing and thinking critically. Without regard for what others thought of me, I immediately removed myself from the HIV paradigm, from my doctors, and from everybody who would not believe what I was telling them: that HIV is a lie and there is no HIV. I was a lone survivor screaming out to others to save themselves by listening to me, researching the dissenting perspective about HIV and removing themselves from a campaign that would eventually kill them, while profiting others.

I loved me enough to do that. You can too. You can be a Rainbow Warrior!

My intuition revealed, "Wherever you place your feet is your home that I, *Goddess Kundalini*, have given you." Ascending through the heart chakra of unconditional love, you learn to commit to your spiritual practice, face your fears, stop kidding yourself and really change, thus relieving your conscience.

I do not mean changing what you consider to be bad habits. I mean changing your consciousness to the realization that there is nothing to do in life but love. Love does it all. If you relax on the axes of the wheels of life, you will re-experience health. The chakras are the wheels of life. Use knowledge and awareness of the chakras to bring light into your inner world and then radiate divine love out into the universe.

Alas! You have realized that love is divine power. You have ascended the chakra column from embodiment of the lower chakras and are now at the midway point between the lower and higher self on your way to enlightenment of the upper chakras, where reside higher spiritual awareness and spiritual ability. You are now in the heart and power of divine love in action, where opposites merge, and you have an opportunity to heal issues of love, grief, loneliness, fears of betrayal, jealousy and hatred though a consciousness of unconditional love. Intending and healing this center is possible when you realize that, in truth, love is divine power.

Blue, Throat Chakra, Surrender Personal Will To Divine Will

Blue is the color of the throat chakra, the center of expression positioned in the throat in the area between the 3rd and 5th cervical vertebra. Its element is sound. You must be able to speak and hear the truth. As you commit to the higher self as opposed to your lower nature, you intend to communicate with others freely and creatively instead of lying to them or stifling your own expression for whatever reason. Imbalance in this chakra can lead to manifestations of sore throat and other throat problems like laryngitis. There may be an inability to speak up to authority which can cause energetic imbalance a lead to illnesses like gingivitis, dental issues and even Colds.

The simplest way to know which chakra governs a body part is to note the position of the chakra and its closeness to the body part. When a person receives an HIV+ diagnosis s/he might believe themselves or others to be a potential sexual contaminant. S/he might begin to lie to other people to protect their own reputation. Many people hide their diagnosis from others fearing HIV Stigma and the reactions dismissive or hurtful attitudes of others. Finding a way to express yourself with integrity by surrendering personal will to the will of the divine is the lesson of the throat chakra.

I love to sing. Singing out loud, "acapella" makes me happy. It is special for me to bring a song to life and express it in my own unique way without instrumental backup. Each of us is born with a means of expressing ourselves. I actually found the courage within myself to sing "Bridges" by (Dianne Reeves), and speak at a private party and benefit for the "AIDS Walk" in Atlanta. The highest compliment I received the night of my performance was from a lovely lady who said she would never forget that night. She said, "You have a quality about you that is like indeed special, like Jesus." She went on to say, "Your sharing with us will be on peoples' minds as they lie down to go to sleep tonight." The universe works in mysterious ways. Her loving comments gave me a boost of energy that will last forever.

Healthfulness of the fifth chakra, the throat chakra, is related to how honestly you express yourself, and open to the opportunity to surrender your personal will to the will of the divine by letting go of old notions about who or what you are. When you are dishonest, your body and mind is violated. There were times when I violated my mind and body by not being true to myself. As a result, I hated myself deep within. I had lost total acceptance of myself.

Without a doubt the greatest barrier I built to loving myself was that I knew that it would be necessary to share my most intimate horror; the horror of thinking of myself as a possible murderer. Both before and after receiving an HIV+ diagnosis, I never had sex with the intent of hurting another person. All I ever wanted was the love of another to make me feel better about myself, and to make the other person enjoy the experience. I sometimes, however, disdainfully felt myself worthy of death because I thought that I might have been responsible for possibly passing the alleged HIV virus to another whenever I had sex, even so-called "protected sex." I could not rationalize being sexually intimate without possibly being the cause of someone else's demise. "Safe" and "safer sex" for me carried no real meaning.

In my mind, using condoms could not possibly keep me from spreading the disease to others or having another infect me. If I kissed another, I worried that I had passed the virus to the other person and vice versa. Even when someone expressed an interest in having a friendship relationship with me, I always found ways to push him/her away. I unconsciously started arguments to create division. I refused to allow anyone to get close to me. I became so insecure that I did not believe I was worthy of a life of love. A perfect date could become a disaster without warning just as I had subconsciously planned, even though I may have at times been unconscious of precipitating it.

Back when I worried about dying from HIV, my thinking was "inflamed" in almost every waking moment of the day and night. I now know why many so-called HIV+ people often succumbed to meningitis, which caused swelling and pressure of the brain and spinal cord. The swelling and pressure was the result of inflamed thinking. Constant fear, self-loathing, uncertainty and worry were at the root of such dis-eases. I saw my body's response to that kind of thinking, that ill-state of consciousness. The skin discoloration of my spinal column revealed it. The necessity of popping my neck and cracking my back to release tension became an awful ritual. I had to free up some space within, lighten up and release feelings and emotions that were bogging me down from guilt, shame and worry.

Listen to your body.

The only solace came when I rationalized that my carefully chosen sex partners were promiscuous and were just as *at-risk* as I was. Maybe they were re-infecting me. After all, none of us could be certain if we were so-called HIV+. We were advised and urged to test for HIV regularly. The sheer confusion around what it actually meant to be HIV+ was draining energy from my body and my spirit and left me tense. We sometimes said in our culture and community that, "It's a small gay world." You would often here on the grapevine that the person you had slept with had also slept with his friends or associates. I supposed that some measure of comfort could be taken in the randomness of it all.

Stemming from all the confusion, a hole was left inside me, an emptiness that seemingly could not be filled, until the *Christ* in me through the grace of *Holy Spirit/Mother God Kundalini* awakened and healing was made manifest.

I know that I am not the only one to have endured thoughts and feelings of self-loathing. Back then, potential sex partners would scan and scrutinize your whole body before getting physically close to you--as if to look for signs of "the virus", perhaps a rash or sore of some sort, or maybe discoloration of the skin. We would then decide to avoid each other if we thought the other person was contaminated. God forbid if anyone had gone on a diet and had lost weight.

Sex in the dark became a thing of the past. The act itself became so impersonal. We were valued by the appearance of our body, not for who we are. Suddenly, we were off to a gym to try to sculpt a near perfect specimen. We spent hours in the sauna after hearing reports of how a doctor had warmed the blood of an AIDS patient and supposedly

THERE IS NO HIV

killed some of the virus in the process. How ridiculous is that kind of thinking?

The conspiracy to confuse and kill had effectively taken hold and was going as planned. It still is to this day, but in my opinion is beginning to fade in the light of expanded consciousness. Illegal drug highs and indiscriminate sex (illusions) were deceivingly pleasing physical measures that soothed the guilt and shame over being who you are.

All drugs are toxic to the body. Using them is no recipe for healthful living.

There is not a shred of evidence that is both tangible and reliable to prove without a doubt that the so-called HIV virus is contagious and spread by body fluids, although, there are research studies that show that groups who wear condoms have lower rates of purported so-called HIV infection. If you change the name from acquired immune deficiency to "auto"-immune deficiency, the very label "auto" should cause a serious "aha" moment. HIV and AIDS would necessarily mean that a person self-inflicted the so-called disease on themselves.

It was as if I had opted out of this lifetime because I did not love myself anymore and blamed myself for the possible loss of other lives.

Interestingly, there are studies that purport that those persons sharing needles while using drugs are infected at higher rates, along with people who work in the sex industry. Can you think of any groups of people more disrespected and hated in our society, as perpetuated by certain media than drug users and sex workers? Purported research statistics ostensibly showed HIV cases among these groups have declined since 1996. This is in direct opposition to what we were being told by the media and HIV outreach groups.

I am astounded that it matters not that the fallout from the "sexual fear epidemic" would eventually affect those not in these groups. But fear is far reaching. It can find its way into the tiniest of crevices in the hearts of those who have television as their best friends: those who become engrossed in whatever they hear or read, particularly if it is of a negative nature. If a television news reporter told you that your mother was an ax murderer, you would probably doubt that she was the saint you always knew. The slightest hint of moral imperfection in a person, suggested by the media, can precipitate hostility towards both the meekest and mightiest of individuals. Purported HIV infection has become pandemic as a result of the spreading of worldwide sexual fear.

As God would have it, light would be brought into the dark room. People like me are becoming aware of their own ability to be masters of their own fate. Many of my friends who were experiencing debilitating direct-effects from prescribed, highly-toxic drugs, stopped at once and are doing better than ever.

I never had an HIV disease. No one gave me HIV, nor did I ever give a lethal disease to anyone else. Any symptoms of disease that I ever had were indicative of my consciousness and were not in any way related to the presence of an elusive particle known as HIV which was never proved to exist.

Dr. Nancy Turner-Banks, MD, in her compelling, world-acclaimed book, *Aids, Opium, Diamonds and Empire: The Deadly Virus of International Greed*, said just as I had previously determined:

o   "Whatever the HIV antibody test is measuring it is not sexually transmitted, nor is it necessarily lethal."
o   Further, she said that there is no AIDS or HIV disease-there are twenty-nine already existing diseases, with various

etiologies, that have been clumped together in people who develop symptoms of AIDS after testing HIV positive.

o   Only those who have a positive HIV antibody test will be said to have the AIDS disease; whereas those with a negative HIV antibody test will have whatever the diagnosis happens to be--even though in reality they both have the same disease. For example, positive HIV antibody test plus (+) tuberculosis equals (=) AIDS; negative HIV antibody test + tuberculosis = tuberculosis.

"I am the Master of my fate. I am the captain of my soul" –Invictus

Intrusive attempts to manipulate human consciousness notwithstanding, the fear, hopelessness and death campaign generated a climate of closeness and togetherness among all the peoples of the world. It has generated a spirit of "unity." Do you "feel" me?

I love going to social events and seeing brothers and others I have not seen in years who are alive and well. There is an unspoken language of love born out of suffering. No need for words, we hug. No need to check our watches and cell phones, or to conveniently look the other way when we pass on the street. We embrace. We support. We understand. We know. We have withstood and thrived in a world that largely stood against us. We tacitly acknowledge that we are here by divine right.

There is not one of us whose life has not been touched by the death or sickness of a loving friend, lover or family member impacted by an HIV+ diagnosis, death by prescription. It is not because we are all wearing "body condoms" that we are still alive. Many are sustained temporarily by prescribed drugs they believe to be creating health in their body. Others instinctively know the power of the love of God and the love of self.

I am not a murderer. I am love.

The real murderers

The murderers might be the "bible-toting-righteous-and-proud-church-going-do-gooders" who preach division and hate in the name of God, yet turn away those searching for God's refuge and loving care. The murderer's might be those who proclaim that HIV is homosexuals' deserved punishment. The murderers might be the greedy media moguls, who spread fear and misinformation about HIV. The murderers might be the scientists who forge inconsistent and false medical research regarding DNA, virology, immunology, retroviruses, etc. in order to keep research dollars flowing into their pockets.

It is a known fact that there are over one hundred factors that could yield a false-positive result to a so-called HIV antibody test. The money-hungry, legal-lethal-drug-dealers violate the human body with toxic chemicals that do more harm than good, while extending their profit margins until a person's body gives way to physical death. The murderers might be those who slight and slander homosexuals and others in hopes of elevating themselves. The murderers might be family and friends who reject their supposed loved ones after hearing the news that they received an HIV+ diagnosis. The murderers might be those who are killing masses of people all over the world and in particular Africa, where *melanated, hue-colored* people are diagnosed with so-called HIV/AIDS, and are killed by prescribed, highly-toxic drugs which include AZT and assorted ARVs, in the name of philanthropy. In Uganda and all over Africa, and in fact the world, people are led like sheep to the slaughter. Africans suffer from poor environmental conditions, malaria, dysentery, diarrhea, pneumonia and mal-nutrition, all of which can be treated, most of which already existed as a result of colonization.

Might you be a murderer?

The best among us are being murdered.

***My late best friend, Everett Rachel, was a Star Trek and science fiction fan and enthusiast. He read voraciously as if looking for the answers to questions about the universe. He had been a celebrated scholar, a National Merit Finalist in high school and a 4.0 student in undergraduate school. He was immediately accepted to University of Alabama (UAB) medical school, attended for 2 years and quit. He relocated to Atlanta, Georgia and accelerated through the ranks of the corporate environment at Roche Biomedical Laboratories where he worked as one of the managers in the HIV Testing Department. The stress that befell him, having to determine whether the vials of blood revealed a death sentence for people, during those days, caused him great stress. Someone convinced him to test for HIV, even though he rarely, if ever even had sex. My late best friend had a complex about being overweight.

Several years later he was murdered by the AIDS Establishment, in my opinion. The HIV+ diagnosis led to severe depression. A friendly, funny, garrulous genius had suddenly become withdrawn. I later learned that he had been seeing a psychiatrist. I thought, "Everett, seeing a psychiatrist? Come on, now! Not Everett." Yes, Everett was also bombarded with both psychotropic drugs and harmful HIV drugs like AZT in the middle 90s. Ingesting all those drugs whose interactions were and still are largely unknown and detrimental, poisoned his body and resulted in his death.

I will always remember the last day I went to see him at the hospice. Other than his big, clear, brown eyes, nothing about him looked like him. His eyes were just as they had always been, clear, bright, and piercing. His body, however, had dilapidated around him. His arms were covered with rashes. His skin felt leathery and wrinkled and made him look aged.

I held his arm, peered deeply into his eyes and told him that I loved him. I told him that I had always loved him, and that I would always love him. He smiled, nodded, and closed his eyes peacefully. I walked out of the death motel and cried all the way home. I cried for him. I cried for his family. I cried for myself and I cried myself to sleep that night and many nights afterwards.

The next day while still at work, I called the hospice to ask about him and was informed that he had died. Years later, after doing all the necessary research, I realized that a living genius had been murdered. I did not cry at his funeral because I had loved him while was alive. Others wailed. His older brother had also been buried a few months earlier, having also been murdered with prescribed, toxic HIV drugs.

In my heart of hearts, I know that it was Everett, through Mother Goddess Kundalini who had led me every step of the way to learning the truth about HIV antibody testing. It was Everett who accompanied me on my journey toward uncovering the HIV conspiracy from beyond the veil of physical death? In a sense, Everett sacrificed his life knowing that I would one day uncover the truth, save myself and share the truth about HIV antibody testing with you and the world, because I am a Rainbow Warrior.***

Genocide and Eugenics

I submit to you that HIV antibody testing targets the best and brightest among us. We are under attack. Something in our DNA sets us apart and targets us for destruction. Let us never cease to find out exactly what the tests are looking to identify, which when it finds whatever it is, people are then diagnosed HIV+ and targeted for destruction, and are murdered with poisonous drugs.

Today, even children in the womb are under attack with prescribed toxic drugs and vaccines given to pregnant mothers who were diagnosed HIV+. Pregnant mothers themselves are murdered. Children are murdered. Teens are murdered as are adults. Please, **wake up** and stop these murders and the murderers. They tried to murder me. They could not kill me but they succeeded in cutting off my penis, a-modern-day-lynching, metaphorically speaking. They succeeded by disrupting my entire adult life and halting my sexual freedom. Heterosexual males who are diagnosed so-called HIV+ experience this metaphorical lynching too; that is; if they live to tell about it.

I am alive and thriving today, and I will continue to do all I can to investigate and get to the bottom of this crisis. The lives of the slain, nor mine, shall have been lived in vain.

I am responsible for the lives of others in that I love them and help them experience self-love, which in turn increases my love for myself. (Blow Horn). God humbled me so that I could be opened me to divine love. *Mother/ Father God* loved and taught me to love myself. I am open to Spirit. I live my life finding ways to show love to every person I meet. I am a Rainbow Warrior!

> Oh Great Spirit, Whose voice I hear in the winds and Whose breath gives life to all the world, hear me.
>
> I come before You, one of Your many children. I am small and weak. I need Your strength and wisdom.
>
> Let me walk in beauty, and make my eyes ever behold the red and purple sunset. My hands ever respect the things You have made, my ears sharp to hear Your voice.
>
> Make me wise so that I may know the things You have taught my people, the message You have hidden in every leaf and rock.
>
> I seek Your strength not to be superior to my brother, but to be able to master myself.

Make me ever ready to come to You with clean hands
and straight eyes, so when life fades as a fading sunset,
my spirit may come to You without shame.

--Chief Yellow Lark

Open your throat chakra by being honest about your life. Refuse to
allow fear to keep you from being you. Express who you are in every
aspect of your life. Remember that lying violates the mind and body.
Free yourself from the shackles of mental, bodily and spiritual slavery.
Create loving thoughts. Speak and hear with love. Share your body
using loving gestures and give thanks to the Creator for all that you are.

Look into the mirror and say aloud seven times, "(Your Name), be
who you are. Love yourself."

You are someone special.

In this writer's opinion, the cycle of life is thus perpetuated, until
each and every soul is back from whence it came, in actuality where it
is already, immersed in *The Most High God*. You are one with the *Source
of All That Is*. You are one with *The Most High God* right now. But you
are not aware of it, nor do you understand its implications for health
and healthful living. Love yourself the way you are and become all you
want to be.

The irony is that there is no irony. As I wrote this book and
ascended through the chakras, the universe lovingly brought me
situations to transcend, in order that my words were expressions of
truth. Everything in life happened in "divine order." There were no
coincidences. There were no mistakes. I chose to listen to my feelings
from moment to moment, and to act on what was right for me in
present time, and allowed light to illuminate the darkness.

Being honest about having received an HIV+ diagnosis has been challenging, to say the least. It seemed that whenever I shared with others my research and experiences with my so-called diagnosis and subsequent healing experience, I was frequently met with opposition. People seemed to think that I was deluding myself if I thought for one second that my views were going to help anyone better understand the disease. I disagreed.

For over 17 years and counting, people have not doubted that I believe that I am healed, yet they warn that I am risking my life by not taking my prescriptions. They ask me my viral load, t-cell and cd-4 count. I can hardly keep from laughing right in their faces most of the time, but I compose myself and refrain from mocking them as best I can.

Many of them go on to claim that they knew others just like me who stopped taking their prescriptions, and succumbed to "the virus", another of those terms that people adopt when they have allowed themselves to be conditioned and programmed with a language of death. "There is no HIV" I tell them and they look at me as if I have lost my mind. I welcome intelligent conversation and friendly debate, yet rarely ever seem to get anything other than restatements of propaganda. I have yet to meet a staunch HIV believer to debate me scholastically about the issue and win convincingly. I always win. They cannot win because they cannot show evidence for the isolation and purification of a so-called HIV virus from the very beginning. Yes, they can provide all sorts of erroneous subsequent so-called scientific evidence concocted by people siphoning research dollars while pretending to really care. They are the well-meaning philanthropists. They ought to be ashamed of themselves. None of what they ever do makes any sense to me. People only know what they have heard on television or read in some gay publication. Heck the doctors only pretend to know and instead follow orders or risk losing their positions

Nobody has ever shown me proof of purification and isolation of so-called HIV.

The really ridiculous part is when people start saying, "I've seen it." I've seen it under the electron microscope", or some other ridiculous notion like that. All they have seen is a television news report with actors clad in lab coats, wearing goggles and gloves with beakers and test tubes everywhere in the background, and maybe a microscope or two on the counter. Then they see the camera switch to a slide of cellular debris with an arrow pointing to dead cellular material that they label "the virus". The whole thing is absurd.

People are so gullible that they think they need the approval of their trained killers who often do little other than write prescriptions, and who know little to nothing about healing and alternative healing modalities, of which there are many, the unwitting fall for just about anything a person wearing a "white-coat" tells them. That is not a good idea at all.

When I realized that my doctor knew very little of what he was talking about regarding HIV, I removed myself from his co-called care and never looked back. That was over 17 years ago. If you did not get it the other times I mentioned it, let me say it to you again. I removed myself from their so-called care and treatment over 17 years ago and never looked back. I am so glad to be me, as critical thinker and researcher. I do not readily fall for other people's insanity. Doctors would literally have killed me had I allowed them to continue destroying my nervous system and my spirit. They would have treated me right into the graveyard or crematorium, after stealing the organs from my dead body.

Let me state clearly, that I do not encourage or advocate any persons' refusing prescribed drugs unless they choose to do so. I stopped my prescriptions because of their detrimental effects to my health and quality of life. I had begun to experience numbness in my toes and fingers. I could not rationalize continuing prescribed drugs that were negatively impacting my health, destroying my nervous system. My intuition led me to make a personal decision to cease all prescribed drugs. I am alive today for having made that critical decision. I knew many who continued them and died. Yet, I only know few people today who believe they are being helped by their prescribed HIV drugs.

More importantly, I "knew" that love would heal me. I did not just believe it would happen, I knew in my heart that it would happen. I just did not "know" when it would happen. My healing took place as an event in time during meditation, and was not merely the result of wishful thinking.

Let love be your guide. Divine love and love of self, my higher self, shepherds me.

I have shared and believe it to be imperative to thank the universe within for any illness that arises. Illnesses are red flags that alert you to self-created ill-thinking patterns. Illnesses provide a road map to recovery health. So-called HIV taught me self-love and to release shame and guilt over being myself, a homosexual, same gender loving, black man. So-called HIV taught me that I am loved as I am. And to love myself just as I am. As is said, "If the *Supreme Creator of All That Is,* is for me, then who can be against me?"

I learned that when ***"self" and "not-self" become "con-fused"***, the flaw is exposed: the flaw being "denial of self", based on sexual shame and guilt. Bodily illness helped heal flaws of my soul by exposing those flaws. I had created distortions in my being by not loving myself. I was ashamed of my sexuality and felt guilty for being me. There was no way for me to be healthy because I was not complete within myself.

In effect, manifestations of illness in my body was one of the ways *Goddess Kundalini* transformed me. She insisted that I love myself, all of me. I came to treat myself with love, respect and kindness, rather than judgment and pathology.

I let go into uncertainty, but with complete faith in the divine in me to heal me, trusting that my basic nature and that of the world are not different. The threat of death became a liberating opportunity in which my sadness became my joy. Realization of these truths restored vital energy to my body, vital energy that nourishes every particle of my being and create health in my body.

Disease (dis-ease with oneself) is a process of liberation. You get to see yourself as you really are. As it were, the flaw is exposed. It allows you to consider your relation to the divine in yourself. Disease manifests in your body when you do not recognize who you really are. You feel cut off from love, because experiences in life have left you feeling that you were incapable of being forgiven for perceived mistakes you made. Dis-ease, in effect, illuminates a direct disconnection in your mind. My energy circuits were not broken. They were misaligned. This was not the *Supreme Creator's* doing. It was mine. This, in truth, is that.

"When the heart is coherent, the body's magnetic field is allowed to get its instructions from the soul." (Mierzwicki, Interview with Dan Winter)

Die daily to fear. Live in love and recognize that you are divine. Death by murder from ARVs is not in keeping with the principle of surrendering personal will to divine will. Your higher self knows that within you is the ability to ascend to the level of honesty where truth in expression and to the realization of your worthiness allows you to become divine voice.

I am divinely guided, guarded and protected, at all times. You are too.

Indigo, Third-Eye Chakra,
Seek Only the Truth

The Third Eye Chakra, also known as the "First-Eye," is located in the center of the forehead slightly above and between the eyebrows. Indigo is the associated color and light is the element of the 3rd Eye Chakra. When your third-eye is balanced and open, you gain knowledge insight and wisdom into any given situation because you are able to see clearly the past, present and future. Untruths and deception surrounding the HIV hoax can lead to imbalances not only in people diagnosed so-called HIV+, but also within and among the masses that have tell-lie-vision as their best friend. If people do not watch, read, or listen discerningly they are highly suggestible to being manipulated and mind-controlled.

Does anybody truly love you? Do you truly love anyone? Do you love yourself? Does *Mother/Father God* love you?

You know intuitively that the answer to these questions is a resounding "Yes!"

Energy of the third-eye chakra is generated by the heart chakra. Through the third eye/ajna chakra the force that generates the third eye on the spiritual level, you extend your perception and see beyond the illusion of limitation and ordinary reality. You see beyond the *"Veil of Isis,"* the veil of illusion.

Ordinary reality appears as duality: darkness and light, opposites as up and down, here and there, good and bad, male and female, the creator and the created. In the third eye you have the opportunity to glimpse the divine. You come to the realization of God in all, and can see beyond the veil of illusion (duality), and create (unity) in and among all life.

Everyone has experienced rejection and acceptance, been the judge and judged by others, used and the user, loved and hated, the lover and the hater.

Recall to mind the illustration of the caduceus at the beginning of this chapter. The wings are positioned after the sixth, third-eye chakra, at the intersection of the snakes? The snakes on caduceus represent the polarity of opposing forces in nature. At this juncture you have the potential to *fly* from *embodiment* to *enlightenment* to the Godhead, through *"unity consciousness."*

Having experienced both polarities, you now the opportunity to learn compassion for the darker side of yourself and others. By embracing and forgiving your own *dark side*, the need to exhibit extreme negative behaviors become a thing of the past. When you repress your darker nature you create a false persona or image to show the world. That false image hides the true soul or true person that you are and can cause dis-ease with self. An example of this sometimes manifests as addiction, the result of running from your true nature, in all facets of self-expression.

At the 3rd-eye, you can become *"Christed,"* "crystalline". All masks and images are peeled away and full expression of emotions results in a new sense of aliveness and creative expression. This leads to the ability to embrace and experience the joy and celebration of life along with an ability to feel and move your pain, anger and fear.

Energy rising from the heart chakra allows unconditional love to flow freely and lets two or more hearts connect with a new sense of community, harmony and equality among all in existence as well as a new form of relationship with others, nature and God.

The *"Christ-ed"* individual recognizes that all expressions of truth are valid and learns not to condemn others for having their own individual experiences with reality. No one truth is superior to another truth and all personal truths are valid in God's grand scheme.

When you look into the eyes of a stranger or someone you think you hate, you see yourself. You literally see a reflection of yourself when you look deeply into the eyes of another. You know you are truly filled with love when you accept that you are seeing yourself. You are seeing (g)od.

Look into your own eyes and the eyes of anyone you encounter with unconditional love.

Your soul is said to reside in the third-eye chakra. As it is close to the crown chakra, which is pure undifferentiated energy (spirit), it marks the first movement away from the *Divine* through the heart chakra to the lower chakras. Similarly, it is the final point before reunion with the *"Source" of All That Is*. It ascends through the heart of love to the upper chakras of "higher self" toward unity and oneness with the *Holy Spirit*.

There is power in realizing that you can see in another person whatever you choose to see.

Also referred to as the eye of the divine, the third-eye chakra is the doorway to expanded consciousness and extra-ordinary vision. From the brow area, consciousness projects images onto the "mind screen" and one can simply observe the images or act upon them as an interpretation of reality.

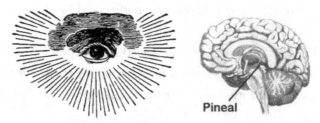

Pineal

Those creating so-called HIV+ symptoms in their body are self-evaluative and are looking for truth. I had looked for feelings of adequacy from others. I had tried to find meaning in my life and clarity of purpose. Understandably, I had become a mental slave to all the negativity surrounding the HIV controversy.

As well, I had allowed myself to become imprisoned by my lower chakras. Ill-thinking generated energy dissension and depletion. I had longed to feel a love supreme. I longed to be accepted just as I am. Astonishingly and astoundingly, I was brought to the amazing realization that I had created the experiences of physical illness, because I related to the world without self-realization. Ultimately it was me who had denied my (g)od-self.

"Dis-ease" with myself settled into my consciousness (my thinking). "Disease" in my body had settled into my physical vehicle (my body), and began to manifest as illness.

That was when I decided no, no, no, not me, not me, not now, not ever. That is when I said, *"Headaches, be gone. Dogmatism, go away. Skepticism, hit the road, take grief with you, take shame and guilt too, and don't forget to take away worry and doubt. While you're at it, take fear. Bring me self-love and adoration."*

Needless to say I am finding a new sense of contentment by infusing my dark areas with the light of unconditional love. Love of self and all others. Love of all that is. True freedom lies here. *The greatest thing you'll ever learn is just to love and be loved in return."* Remember "Nature Boy" sung by Nat King Cole? If I can just do that, I can re-member my fragmented soul. This was the lesson of the third eye-chakra. From the 3rd-eye, your life has the ability to take flight. You are now ready to soar. *"Can you take your broken wings and learn to fly?"*

Experiences provoked me to the realization that my thoughts created my world. I tortured myself when I clung to the illusion of duality, when I continued to see choices I made as mistakes, when I looked around every corner for the wrath of a punishing God. I had persisted in my conditioning to believe that some evil force existed in the world and was doing battle with good. I figured that all I had to do was determine my relation to it, align myself with "all good" and experience the blessings of the universe. If I could only have found the secret dwelling place of the *Most High* within myself, I would somehow have transcend the suffering.

As Above So Below.

In truth, you are a world unto yourself. Your outer reality is a reflection of your inner world.

When questions as these arise in your mind, remind yourself that you are loved by God no matter what you do.

Having embraced your shadow, you can choose to turn from darkness to light; light being awareness that God is a creator of infinite possibilities. As you make your move through life's daily challenges you are now compelled to assert your truest self with most people. You expect that they will accept you for all that you are.

I detest how violent, gay-bashers try to justify their hateful and barbaric behavior by saying that the person they attacked flaunted his/her sexuality and deserved what s/he got, as if s/he had no right to be who s/he is. Because of awareness, I simply feel the feelings of anger toward homosexual bashers, and generate appropriate ways of expressing, and releasing them, in order that I maintain health. I love me even when others do not, and love others in spite of themselves.

Why are so many straight people in opposition to homosexuality? The answer probably partially lies in the understanding of "contagious group think." Is their conditioning so strong that they simply cannot help hating homosexuals? I think not. Are you wrong in believing that God loves you even when others do not seem to? No. That would be unwise. Will your entire life be one big search for acceptance from others? No, as long as you choose to create it differently.

I sometimes felt so alone. Even within the SGL/Homosexual/Gay community I felt isolated. So many Same Gender Loving/Homosexual/Gay people live in fear, because of their own sexuality. They downplay their own confidence and scandalized those who do not. I am not like every other same gender loving person. Must homosexuals be my only companions? If it is true in my mind, I will give it life. Am I off my rockers for believing that so-called HIV has nothing to do with AIDS and is not spread through sexual contact? I don't think so. I am the living proof. Is health really generated through love of God, self, and all others, and everything in existence? The answer is an unequivocal yes. This is the only way for me to mend holes in my heart.

As you grapple with these obstacles to transformation, constantly invoked the principles of the chakras: namely, the principle of seeking and expressing only the truth, your truth, the truth being that love exists in all. You simply do not have to be swayed by the beliefs of others. You are now compelled to love them in spite of themselves, or better yet, despite their views of you. Love yourself in spite of yourself. That, is inner love.

Inner-love is accomplished through the power of distinguishing between **"Self"** and **"Not-Self."** In other words, you must ask, "Who am I? And who am I not?" Know that there is not a spot where God is not, and there, you are. You are an integral part of the creation of love "just- as –you- are." Accept yourself. Unconditionally love yourself.

You are creating your own physical symptoms of disease, your own illnesses.

I would like to elaborate how I have come to accept whatever happens in my life as a creation of my own doing; in particular, how that relates to taking full responsibility for creating physical symptoms of disease as well as breaking free of them. I shall one day die a physical death. But I do not have to die today from being poisoned by prescribed, highly-toxic drugs (ARVs).

I've already stated that my healing took place, was an event in time, and was not the result of mere wishful thinking. I believe it was a result of love and grace, and my desire to ascend, and love all of me, despite what others said would be my fate for "choosing" to be homosexual. I also know that it

> *is possible to for me to create the same tensions in my body and the resulting inhibited energy flow that resulted in the manifestation of physical disease.*

Any disease manifested in my body was a result of my moving my thinking away from the divine in me. Though often times done unconsciously, it was my thinking that caused my body to respond.

Louise L. Hay's *"You Can Heal Your Life"* was and still is an invaluable resource I use to heal myself whenever I experience any illness which I now know is related to my own ill-state of consciousness, not from a non-existent HIV virus. Her book offers the metaphysical causes of disease along with affirmations to realign your consciousness so that you can self-heal your dis-eases.

I created my own physical symptoms of illness:

- Conjunctivitis (anger and frustration at what I was seeing in life), as I mentioned earlier and
- Diarrhea (fear, rejection, running-off)
- Athletes foot (frustration at not being accepted),
- Jock itch (itching to get out or away),
- Cold (mental confusion and disorder or too much going on at once/improper diet),
- Inflammation (seeing red, inflamed thinking and fear),
- Headache (invalidating myself and self-criticism),
- Congestion (response to mass negativity and belief in statistics) and
- Low-back pain (lack of financial support),
- Night sweats (anger running-off)
- Swollen lymph glands (inability to re-center one's mind on the essentials of life, joy and love), all which stemmed from my internal states of being.

When I experienced physical symptoms and discomfort of any kind, I used meditation to observe my energy in the chakras periodically throughout the day and night. In particular, after having sexual intercourse, I took the time to feel my energy in the lower chakras, root, and sacral and solar plexus. If I felt constriction of life force energy in an area of my body, I consciously chose to relax and release it while affirming love and good in my life in order to restore energetic balance, health and wellness.

I closely examined thoughts and feelings I had had during day-to-day living of life; actions and reactions during interactions with people. Emotions, fantasies, dreams and nature were all food-for-thought, all of which led me back to the understanding that my emotional make-up, fears, and personality traits all have their rightful place in this world and in my development.

I realized that I have a right to be a character on the stage of life. I will never be ashamed to be me.

Self-Pity:

> *"I never saw a wild thing sorry for itself. A small bird will drop frozen dead from a bough never having felt sorry for itself."*
> ~~*D. H. Lawrence*

Another point I would like to make before proceeding further, is that all life is contradiction. Implicit in contradiction is duality, right and wrong, good and evil. But in truth, love is all there is. Can one know freedom without the experience pain? Is it not pain that sets us free? The illusion is that there is right and wrong and good and evil. The truth is that love is all there is.

Love is all there is. Love itself is the reason that we must love ourselves. We should also love others. We should be more like the *Supreme Creator* of all that is, was or ever will be; pure love, unified, undifferentiated, undisputed, spirit; the all.

Away from the darkness of HIV madness and into the light, utilizing divine sight! There is no HIV! You are free!

> "...On the wings of love up and above the clouds,
> the only way to fly."
>
> ~~Jeffrey Osborne

Hence, the lesson of the sixth, 3rd eye chakra is ascension into the divine, though we live and breathe in a world of duality. Let the pain and threat of so-called HIV set you free, as it did me. Seek only the truth. You have ascended your lower nature through the heart of unconditional love and your throat center of unconditional truth. You now ascend to the 3rd-eye chakra where male and female energies become one. In the state of non-dual consciousness you develop your psychic powers, for instance, clairvoyance, your ability to see the past, present and future clearly. You can become the *knower*. When you seek only the truth your consciousness aspects of cognition, conation and affection allow you to become divine.

Violet, Crown Chakra, Live In the Present Moment of Awareness

The crown chakra is associated with the color violet, and is located at the anterior frontal part in the top part of the head. Thought is its element. The crown chakra is associated with the energies of unity and oneness which is the height of spirituality, when all thoughts are balanced. *Heru, Horus, Jesus (Lord Amanda, Jeshua Ben Josef), Buddha, Zoroaster, Confucius, St. Germaine, El-Morya, Serapis-Bey,* and other Ascended Masters reside here. They are true MASTERS of themselves. They are one with the *Holy Spirit.*

Peak spiritual experiences allow us to transcend ordinary reality and the physical body. The gifts and powers available to us at this level can eventually become stumbling blocks that must be transcended in order to reach the ultimate goal of (g)od-realization. When properly balanced, the crown chakra opens appropriately to allow a deep sense of peace and tranquility. We realize that we are connected to all living things. Conversely, when a person diagnosed HIV + receives news of an alleged terminal illness from a medical doctor or a home HIV test kit, s/he can immediately begin to live in a consciousness of fear, worry, and doubt, effectively fragmenting their thinking that can lead to headaches, depression, apathy and an inability to learn.

You too can glimpse the divine.

I wanted a lotion or drug to rid rashes from my body. However, removing the rashes without understanding of the root causes of the rashes masked that which needed to be healed; my consciousness of anger and irritation over delays in understanding what was happening in my body and in my life. I attempted to use something outside myself to heal that which was within me, an impossible feat. Healing occurs when you draw out that which exists within yourself, the divine within you. Health comes from within. Health cannot come from outside yourself.

Love in your heart indwells you.

Neither could I heal my addictions, save recognition and acceptance of my own inner power. As it were, the flaw, the lack of love for myself or addiction and self-destructive behaviors were exposed. The perceived necessity of needing something outside myself like alcohol or drugs was an illusion. Running myself, in denial of my personal responsibility, created self-deception and manifested as addiction.

You too can heal your physical symptoms and your addictions that reveal that you are at dis-ease with yourself. Your physical symptoms have absolutely nothing to do with a never before purified and isolated HIV virus. They have to do with your consciousness awareness. Your healing is within you.

Addictions to alcohol and illegal drugs exposed my longing for power, acceptance and love. I had an emotional hunger that caused me to seek love and approval. There was an aching in my heart to be seen as I am, but I was terrified of it because of feelings of low self-worth. Yet they all provided a fantastic opportunity for spiritual growth.

The wise on knows that he himself is the path.
The intelligent one knows that he knows nothing.
Faith and trust are beyond explanation.

As the loving universe would have it, I had a most wonderful experience when I went home for the Thanksgiving holiday one year. I had returned home so many times looking for acceptance and love from my family and hometown friends, only to perceive feelings of awkwardness and rejection. Friends and family were ill-at-ease in conversations, and my fears led to readiness to give up on any hope of salvaging relationships from the past. Not that time.

I challenge you to attempt to reconnect with your roots, your family, your homeboys, your girlfriends and your soul-mates from your old stomping-grounds. They really do miss you. This time, go home, or wherever you go with a new agenda, a new perspective of others' role in your life and a new sense of yourself. You will find that opportunities presented to you will yield only the results that God had already planned for your life. He will use you to grow others, although you might not get the opportunity to realize it in that moment.

The universe works in mysterious ways.

See yourself as connected to those you think do not like you and those who you thought were your adversaries. Honor them and yourself with love by expressing your truest self in the present moment and see the wonders of the universe.

I grew up in Montgomery, Alabama, a courageous city comprised of Black people who were brilliant and tenacious against racism and oppression just as I am in standing up against discrimination, oppression and HIV stigmatization against people diagnosed HIV+.

Remember to abide by the principles of the chakras as you move through your interactions with others. Not everybody will see the world as you do, of course. In fact, one guy told me that since I was a faggot, I might as well put a gun to my head and pull the trigger. I found myself looking in the gun's direction, part of me wishing he would pull the trigger and end the horrors I was living. Ironically, over time as I persisted in being my authentic self and treated him with respect as I do all others, he actually enjoyed my company when he felt safe. I guess he had gotten over the stereotype that all homosexual men are sexually attracted to every man they meet. Or perhaps he had found the courage to assert his own freewill despite the threat of the perception that others would say he was a homosexual or less than a man if he was seen with me.

I considered and admitted to myself that perhaps, I had actually created all those years of separation. All of that pain was an invention of mine, a tool I used to grow myself. Perhaps the threat of dying from so-called HIV was needed to propel my spiritual growth by leaps and bounds. Perhaps, deep within me, I knew that I needed to feel rejection in order to learn to feel acceptance and truly accept myself. Thoughts in my mind had created my world. I had to accept myself before others could accept me.

One childhood friend said, "You went poof." Yes, I went "poof" in mind, my body and my spirit when I experienced rejection for being a homosexual from long-time friends and associates, and certainly after receiving an HIV+ diagnosis.

I have found myself and I AM forever changed. I AM renewed and vivified by my ever- expanding consciousness awareness. I AM thankful that I went through it all. It made me who I AM today. I AM aware of my own divinity.

Choose to live in the present moment of awareness. Like the thousand-petal lotus, you can blossom to your highest potential when you become aware of your connection to your soul and spirit and ascend to the level where you dream your creations into manifestation. You are becoming divine.

My Soul Knows

My Soul Knows
After Here its Home
Self-Realization
Ego Gone

Ignorance: The Universe Really Exists
Yet, The Movie On The Screen Persists.
Everything I See
It's All Me

The Nature Of My Existence Pressures My Mind
God Is Everywhere
No Matter The Kind

Mystical Experience
Serious To Sirius
Traverse The Fall
Transcend All

The Veil Of Illusion Lifted
Physical Senses Evicted
Free From Multiplicity
"One True Reality"

No Action No Reaction
No Praise No Ridicule
No Want Nor Not Want
Earth Was The School

Consciousness Expanded
Christhood The Nod
"Gnothi Saeuthon"
"Know Thyself" As God
~ Damian Laster Aka Kabir Amen Ra Horakhty

You are not a victim. You are a creator.

Do not run away anymore. Heal your past even if it requires nothing more than releasing it and forgiving those whom you perceive wronged you. Disturbances in crown chakra energies restrict divine energy flow. Illnesses manifest when you are withdrawn, depressed and afraid to let go into the sacred void. Longing for something more in your life instead of accepting what is can lead to illness. Feeling alienated from the *Source of All That Is* along with feelings of emptiness can lead to physical dysfunction.

Exercise your faith. Commit to and practice your spirituality. Inspiration, continuity of consciousness and unification with the higher self and higher human personality shall prevail.

Freedom and independence are forces which activate the intellect and awaken a search for wisdom and the desire to improve humanity and the planet we live on.

Know that my efforts in writing this book are for none other than you. I want for you that which I desire for myself; healing in every area of life. God is anchored in you. Be mindful in the present moment and move forward in your life.

Do not allow your thoughts to become your dis-eases. Make continual efforts to live your life in the present moment of awareness rather than blindly holding on to the past and having it dictate your thoughts, words and actions in the now. Know that where you are is right where you are supposed to be in the divine now.

You have made no mistakes in life. You are ever growing your way back to the fullness of that which you really are. Accept it. Love it. Love all of yourself. You are loved as you are.

"Metaphysician, Heal Thyself, Radiate and Spiral" love into the world. Never stop loving and growing. Radiate and spiral love energy from your being out into the world.

> *"I believe I can fly. I believe I can touch the sky. I think about it every day; spread my wings and fly away. I believe I can soar. I see me running through that open door. I believe I can fly. I believe I can fly. I believe can fly; cause I believe in me."*
>
> *~ R. Kelly*

Prayer and Meditation, Relaxation, and the Chakras

"Meditation is the mind that brings the youth." Common,
(Rap artist)

Prayer, meditation and relaxation enhance life. It is in the state of prayer felt in the depths of your heart and "feeling meditation" that you receive ongoing healing from Great Spirit. Relaxing the body and mind is the best way to do that.

Allow your spirit to lead you to the best mediation practice for you. Remember, that you are not your body. Your body is merely a vehicle that allows you to experience this dimension and reality.

Make it your goal to get to the point in meditation when you feel divine love energy resume total control of your being. It might appear to creep up on you as if it was waiting for you to stop looking for it so that it can flourish and break through the waiting gates of heaven in your heart and permeate your fragile fleshly barriers.

Inhale and exhale and bring in the gifts of the cosmos. With each exhalation, consciously release awareness of your physical body by letting it go. Stilling the mind is a prerequisite. If it wanders 299 times, gently bring it back 300 times and focus it back to the thought of love alone. This is not an easy feat initially. The mind's nature is like the air. Be patient with yourself while developing control of your thinking. Focusing on the breath and consciously following its rhythm is one way to do it. Repeating affirmations and mantras is another. Faith in yourself as a (g)od is utmost important.

From an almost trance-like state, become fixed and stayed. You are literally anchored in space and time. Then, wait in great anticipation. If you "let go of your center" it just happens naturally. Usually, as promised, a powerful yet unbelievably gentle, undulating, force lovingly enfolds your body temple and beckons your soul. I suppose there can sometimes be an inkling of fear. Release all fear.

Know intuitively that if you are able to completely let go, your soul will heal. I look forward to even to out-of-body experiences (OBEs) as spirit invites. Just as a flower sits in the love of the sun's rays, I am content, however, to stay grounded here in the physical plane of existence.

Wow! The *Christ Energy* is in me. The *Christ Energy* is in you too. This is the "Revelation"—that you are the Christ potential. Many people think Christ Jesus the man is coming back in the physical form to save them. I think the Christ Energy is coming back spiritually to our awareness of that energy already existing within us. When you grasp this most precious awareness, there will be no limitation to your creations. Be wise and loving in your use of Christ-consciousness energy in you. This is the energy of the divine child, Heru child of Ausar and Auset.

"I Am" A Being Of The Violet Flame. "I Am" The Purity God Desires.

I will not bog you down in meditation procedures and techniques as a wealth of information is available on the subject of meditation. You are in need of self-healing. You need it now and are not required to learn a vast amount of information in order to receive it. I did not need to know them to receive my healing. It was only after I received healing that I developed an insatiable appetite for knowledge. I wanted to gain understanding of what had happened in my body and wisdom to know what was happening in my life. I am thankful for that.

It is not rocket science to be able to ask your soul and spirit to lead you to truth. If knowledge is what you seek, you will be guided through any library's maze of books as well as websites in the Internet kingdom right down to the printed words in ink. Remember, *"Seek and Ye shall find."* Do not, however, become a slave to the printed page. Read discerningly. Take what you need into your head and your heart and leave the rest. The spark of the divine is within you. Search within for your (g)od-self, your *Higher Self.*

The Breath of Life

"Breath is the symbol of life. The deeper the breath, the greater the victory over life-threatening irritants."

Tasneem Hameed

U se the breath to relax your mind and body during meditation. The breath carries you deep inside yourself where you begin to feel your blood pulse, cells and tissues rejuvenate and feel and allow your energy to move in swirling, pulling and tugging sensations.

The breath allows you to *"feel"* and to remember that you are alive. The magnificence of the cosmos without is brought within and balance is achieved. In essence, your being is stretched beyond your physical body out into creation. You can become one with all that is.

While the breath of life is sustained involuntarily, breathe consciously as often as you think to do so when you are awake. Begin to practice consciously taking in air through the nostrils and releasing it through your nostrils as well. Let your breathing be intentional and effortless. Breathe lightly. In fact you should not be able to hear the air moving through your nose. Fill your lungs to capacity, sustain momentarily and release the breath slowly from your body with the intent of releasing all fear, worries, concerns, doubts and troubles.

Repeat as many times as your soul guides you. Always ask for the *white light* of protection during any meditation exercise or breathing session. The breath of life is more powerful than you now know. Be careful and mindful. Listen to your body and follow your intuition.

Learn of meditation techniques by seeking that knowledge. Then let go of your center and wait for your soul. Soul will never fail you if you ask in earnest. Say, "I Am the Light". Focus on the light that you are.

Running Energy

"Running energy" is a process wherein you sit erect with our feet planted firmly but gently on the ground or floor with your palms facing upward resting on your knees. Visualize a brilliant golden light radiating from your body at each chakra position.

Imagine breathing the light that you are from within at each chakra energy field. With your eyes closed see the golden divine light within as it travels up through the root chakra of your body. There, it fills and infuses that area and all of its corresponding body parts with energy and anchors you to Mother Earth with love. While the light is there, ponder the true meaning of *"all is one"* and release all prejudice and separation from your consciousness.

If you feel tension or pain in any area allow your attention to stay focused there. Resist the temptation to pull away from the tension or pain. *"Feel into and then through it"*. Be in awe and thankful for its dissolution.

Then, move your awareness to the sacral chakra and the principle to *"honor one another"* while envisioning the gold or white light cleansing and clearing away any and all blockages. You will feel the energy of light present and swirling in each area as you make your ascent through the solar plexus, heart, throat, third eye and crown chakra thinking at each level of that chakra's principle.

Allow light energy to move through you. Remember, that the principle of the solar plexus chakra is to *"respect yourself"* Of course, *"love is divine power"* is the heart chakra's principle. Your heart will swell with love. At the throat chakra, relax and allow the energy to soothe your place of expression. Know that you must *"surrender personal will to divine will"* to achieve any goal in life. You will experience a slight tightness or pressure, a fullness of head sensation that will dissipate with your letting go. *"Seek only the truth"* is next at the third eye chakra. The freeing task of living life as much as possible in the *"present moment of awareness"* comes next into focus at the crown chakra. Then, release this light energy up and out into the universe.

You are now ready to repeat the process in reverse order. Bring the light back down through your crown chakra into your lower body chakras from the crown of your head, for you are royalty. Visualize the radiating golden light of the *Supreme Creator* descending through the third eye and then the heart chakra. Allow it to move down through the lower chakras of embodiment out of you down into the center of Mother Earth below. You are now grounded and balanced. You are now one with the Supreme Creator through the Holy Spirit.

Take a moment then to feel your awareness being fully in your physical vehicle. Give thanks. Breathe. Know and claim perfect health.

Color Therapy

You are invited to research more about color therapy while practicing this same technique for various physical body illnesses. Simply locate the chakra usually found nearest the ailing body part, breathe and then visualize the color associated with the chakra radiating and spiraling from the center of the chakra out into your aura in every direction. Feel it cleansing and restoring health to your body.

From root to crown the colors of the rainbow are **r-o-y-g-b-i-v (red- orange-yellow-green-blue-indigo-violet)**. Afterwards, always claim perfect health and give thanks for your ability to self-heal. There is so much exciting information to learn about healing yourself or better yet accepting healing that is always available to you. Health is who you really are. Had you not experienced illness, you would never have had the opportunity to learn all the things you now practice. It is your divine right to develop your own safe techniques.

Healthful Lifestyle

Only you know what foods and drink make your body feel energized. Associate natural food colors and relate it to each chakra. I drink fruit and vegetable smoothies daily. Mine are likely to have apples, bananas, carrots, kale, chard, spinach pumpkin seeds, myrrh tea, colloidal silver, liquid kelp, chlorophyll, granola, assorted nuts, chocolate almond milk and water. *You are what you eat.* Living beings need living foods created by the earth. Avoid genetically modified foods.

Suffice it to say that a sufficient amount of water works wonders in the body cleansing and purifying your (g)od technology.

Avoid negative tell-lie-vision. Avoid negative people.

Sage and incense are sweet scents.

Enjoy uplifting and relaxing music. Silence is music to the ears as well.

Moderate exercise cleanses and rejuvenates your entire body system.

Take nature walks while appreciating its immense beauty. Meditate while walking.

Perhaps you desire to learn Yoga techniques to further your spiritual growth and development.

Gain an interest in all things metaphysical.

As you continue your spiritual journey, you will likely be compelled to study your real history and Ancient African Spirituality. You will recognize *"Kemet"*, The Land of the Black, as *Al-Chem-y* and *Chem-istry* and the hidden secrets of *Melanin that will allow you to unlock your ancestral memory in your DNA*. It is the secret intelligence within you that will allow you to do extraordinary things and dawn your super human abilities.

Make new friends by being a friend. Be prepared to lose people you thought were friends. Gladly release them. Never let another person crush your spirit. Nurture yourself. Love your body. Lighten up and allow yourself to be happy. Breathe. Breathe again. Breathe consciously throughout the day and night. Fill your lungs to capacity and release all of the air out of your lungs, repeatedly.

Chant HU. Learn the spiritual art of dreaming. Keep a dream journal

Sing out loud. Laugh. Dance. Be playful. Turn off the TV and radio. Breathe. Again, let your spirit guide you. Trust it and know. I do, and I do. You will too.

You will one day become interested in *Shaktipat* to awaken your Kundalini. Perhaps it has already been awakened within you and you are unaware of the changes that are taking place in your body and in your life, and you are possibly in spiritual crisis. Many people are experiencing this lesser known phenomenon and are misdiagnosed with Schizophrenia because they are experiencing reality in new ways as a result of unleashing of the once dormant, coiled Kundalini energy at the base of the spine.

Kundalini is discussed in greater detail in the next chapter.

As pictured in the caduceus on page 46, this energy is represented by the snakes that lie, coiled 3 ½ times and the base of the spine. Raising this energy from the root chakra to the crown chakra results in illumination, the opening of the third eye, the down pouring of grace (healing), and communion with God.

Typically referred to as the *Second Coming of Christ, the Holy Spirit, Divine Mother Goddess Kundalini* who has lain dormant in the base of your spine is waiting to expand your consciousness and reconnect to the *Source of All That Is* will confirm and testify to the unity of God. You will have been born again. And you will know without a doubt that love is your life, you do not die and there is nothing to fear, for love is eternal.

Your soul and spirit may also guide you to learn about the *Antahkarana* or the building of your "Rainbow Bridge" to connect you to Source.

Knowledge of "Sacred Geometry" might then prompt you to begin *"MerKaBa* meditations" to build your personal spaceship. Learn of your multidimensional self.

You will also continue to learn and better understand the pyramids which were built among other things to assist the planet in her ascension into the fourth dimension and beyond and left by your ankh-estors to remind you of your divine potential when the time would come to re-member who you really are. Yes, the pyramids were built by Africans who traveled all over the world.

Again, The Temple of Luxor reveals the "The Temple in Man" and the spiritual centers (chakras) in the human body. You will learn that all knowledge proceeded from the progenitors of culture and civilization in Kemet, "The Land of The Black". Your ankh-estors knew the secrets and power of melanin.

You might also seek extraterrestrial, cosmic and galactic help from our space brothers and sisters. One such group is the Arcturians. The Medical Assistance Program (MAP Teams) can help you heal while you are sleeping, upon request.

Use internet search engines to bring the world to your fingertips.

The Golden-Ankh, Phi Ratio. Golden Mean, Golden Flower of Life and mystery of the Sphinx will be revealed to you. "Light Energy" will take on a whole new meaning in your life as you raise the light quotient level of your physical body through proper meditation, relaxation and proper nutrition, as well as with assistance from higher dimensional beings. Learn of the Maharic Seal meditation protection throughout 12 dimensions of consciousness which no harmful earthly technology can penetrate https://www.youtube.com/watch?v=QpjFN-PWxuk.

Turn your bogus HIV+ diagnosis into an opportunity for your spiritual growth. I certainly learned that the most important love is *Self-Love*. There is an exciting world inside you waiting to be discovered. Remember, when the student is ready the teacher will appear. Be a teacher for others that the universe sends to you. Pay it forward. Observe synchronous events. There are no mistakes.

Now is your time to take back your power from the HIV hoax designed to thwart the evolution of your consciousness, but which presented you with the opportunity to evolve yourself spiritually.

Because we learned, we forgive. Now it is time to teach.

It is my hope that the Black, so-called "conscious" community will soon stop allowing their disdain for homosexuality to cloud their good judgment and ability to think critically about the HIV issue and work to stop the genocide and eugenics campaign against our people. I hope all people of the world wake up and work to end all present atrocities.

Use me as your inspiration. I and many others are the **living proof** that there is no HIV. HIV is a hoax.

Free Yourself! I freed myself over 17 years ago. You can do it too.

You are a Rainbow Warrior!

Kundalini

Kundalini

"With great power comes great responsibility,
"Those willing to harbor the responsibility,
"Are then accentuated in the power,
"Those unable to harbor the responsibility,
"Will be consumed by the power."

~*Unknown*

"As I lay outstretched in absolute thanks and praise to God for all of me, it was as if I had slipped beyond thought and just existed. Somehow, for a moment in time I quelled the chaotic world within. Without warning, I began to feel a miraculous sensation beginning in my feet and proceeding up my entire being as if playing a melody on my body. I honestly felt like a holograph of myself. I couldn't move. I didn't want to move. What was happening to me? From the soles of my feet to the crown of my head the prickly tingling sensation pervaded my entire being. I lay, as if paralyzed, with my mouth agape and tearful eyes, in total awe at what had just happened. And then came the realization that I had been healed of the dreadful disease I had felt of myself, for far too long. I had been given an opportunity to know self-love as I never had before. After two years of intense research, I realized that the grace of God had descended on me, at birth by water and now by the fire of the Holy Spirit. I learned that I had had a Kundalini Awakening." --Damian Q. Laster aka Kabir Amen RA Horakhty (The Rainbow Warrior: Healing HIV through Chakra Awareness, 2001)

This section is written with references in APA style for your benefit and further study.

From that very moment in time in the year 1998, my life changed in ways I could never have imagined. I went "From HIV to Kundalini" and awakened the *Divine Feminine* within. What I initially thought was the grace of God healing me from the threat of physical death from an HIV+ diagnosis turned out to be so much more than healing a physical disease.

> *"The power of Kundalini lies in the actual experience. It goes right into the heart and extends your consciousness so you may have a wider horizon of grace and knowing "the truth"".*
>
> *Yogi Bajhan*

Who knew that what I had initially been taught as a child under a patriarchal system, which wrote the Divine Feminine out of history and represented the *Holy Trinity as The Father, Son and Holy Spirit*, was more correctly represented as *Father God, Mother God, and The Child of God?* The dual aspect of both the masculine and feminine principles had been intentionally misrepresented in favor of forming a patriarchy.

Little did I know then that there was the potential that "…the energy rises upwards, towards your head, and shall awaken your *Kundalini* and become Gods" (Weor, 2009). I did not know immediately what had happened to me, but I found out. I also learned that in Ancient African Spirituality there are the main characters of Ausar, Auset and Heru, who were later renamed Osiris, Isis and Horus, by the Greeks.

When Kundalini awakens, *"The Soul, the consciousness within every individual being has to be torn apart and scattered, through identification with the desires, cravings and ignorance of the ego-personality, and must be reconstituted through spiritual practice in order to have full insight." (Ashby, 2005).*

I had spent a life yearning for something more, something else; something that I thought I didn't already have. As a result of my life-changing Kundalini Awakening (KA), my perception of reality changed in ways I did not know were possible. Little did I know that I could choose to live in the present moment of awareness and affirm my own innate good-ness. I could live in recognition as the Christ Intelligence within, the divine son of my true parents, Father/Mother God.

My KA resulted of my dynamic spiritual awakening, I began to experience a powerful presence, a voice that vibrated instructions and spiritual truth, namely that, all illness is illusion. As the *Holy Spirit* energy rose in me I felt a comforting closeness to The Most High God which compelled me to let go of old thought-forms, concepts and attachments.

Kundalini awakening resulted in changes in consciousness that arise within oneself so as to avoid losing perception of my connection with the third dimensional (3D) world.

You, too, shall progress through the alchemical stages of *Spiritual Transformation*, a never ending cyclic and unfolding and process. The stages of alchemy are: *awakening, blackening, crucifixion, resurrection and rebirth*. My search for help and health after receiving an HIV positive diagnosis from a medical practitioner led to this most miraculous and amazing spiritual experience; Kundalini Awakening.

Kundalini Awakening and HIV

During this time of planetary transformation, Mother God led me to the truth about HIV; that, "HIV-positive response means nothing of any relevance to health" (Whitaker, Fleming, 2010). It was as if I was led by an invisible being or force throughout libraries' and bookstores' maze of books as well as sites and articles in the internet kingdom.

Healing from HIV theories and deceptions by educating oneself is paramount. All drugs, whether legal or illegal are toxic to the body. Cleansing the body of toxic prescription or non-prescription drugs through ozone (oxygen) therapy and proper diet is helpful.

Just as we can make ourselves sick pursuant to our beliefs and thought processes, we can also make ourselves healthy by releasing shame and guilt over sex and sexuality.

Life Purpose

It was with great apprehension that I addressed the topic of HIV being the greatest medical hoax of the 21st century. My intuition and research caused me great pain and rejection from various factions in society as well as strife among my family and friends. Attempting to convince people that HIV is a lie has been most difficult since 1998 when I arrived at my conclusions and began sharing them with the world via the internet. On the one hand, many are still in a consciousness that homosexuality is an abomination to God and that homosexual sexual behavior is disdainful and therefore justifies contraction a deadly disease. And on the other, that forwarding such information could endanger peoples' lives by having them release all fear about sexual activity. I, however, based on my personal experiences as well as research believe that sexual energy and other people are not potential contaminants but are opportunities to express love.

Moreover, that this information is part of my life purpose for being on the planet. I am under the direction and auspices of my soul, not any man. It was *Mother God, Auset, Goddess Kundalini, Divine Feminine /*

Kundalini Principle/Mother God/Holy Spirit who both healed me of the dreadful dis-ease of an ill-state of consciousness I had thought of myself. She led me into the light of truth.

Until my last breath, I will bring to the light the horrible atrocities committed against humanity for genocide and the attempt to thwart the evolution of human consciousness through the misdiagnosis of innocent people as HIV+, and the consequent medical malpractice of prescribing toxic drugs which have debilitating effects and often lead to the physical death of the people who ingest them.

The deplorable fact of what Dr. Boyd Graves says is "400 years of systematic eugenics-based/race specific genocide on natural, *melanated* hue-peoples throughout the world and across the globe" will be called into question. http://www.abibitumikasa.com/forums/oppression-afrikans-technologically-scientifically-mathematically/40683-400-years-systemic-eugenics-race-based-genocide.html

Further, I will promote understanding of Metaphysical Science, Spirituality, and the re-awakening of the Divine Feminine in the consciousness of humanity here on planet Earth. Yes, the Divine Masculine Principle is the *active* component in creation, while the Feminine supports our growth and re-emergence into divinity.

As well, there are those who have been misdiagnosed with Schizophrenia, but who are actually experiencing KA signs and symptoms. They can begin to receive more appropriate treatments for their spiritual emergence and spiritual crisis.

In this light, I have expounded how consciousness creates experience and how altering (shifting) one's consciousness can result in restoration of health to the body.

I intend to share knowledge for more healthful living.

I speak from a position research and from personal experience and of "knowing," rather than from "belief," which is derived from accepting what others say or think, as I have "experienced" first-hand not only the signs and symptoms of KA but also the medical and AIDS Establishment's attempt on my life by diagnosing me HIV + in 1996 and subsequently prescribing toxic and deadly drugs, Epivir and Zerit.

I have intentionally not attacked any person(s) or group(s), only presented the facts of research. I do not take a stand against HIV perpetrators. I stand for what I know to be truth; not fighting against, but fighting for.

I humbly recognize and appreciate my journey as it has led me on a search for self which led to spiritual awakening and the resulting and subsequent expansion of my consciousness. An awareness of a non-dual approach to life where there is a merging of opposites at the heart chakra.

As *Divine Feminine* energy continues to awaken humanity, the biggest challenge in the years to come is that there will be an increase in both the pressures to speak one's truth and pressures to remain silent in order to protect ones' self. This will be both an individual and collective choice (The Hathors & Mary Magdeline, 2009).

I speak my truth. The overall effect of this work will enhance love, peace, health, balance, well-being, harmony and compassion, and will help create a world where everyone can feel at home.

"We are approaching not only a millennium of great change in this solar system, but we are also achieving the great ascension of light in this galaxy after battling the dark forces." (Washta, 1994). (V. Essene, Sheldon Nidle GH)

The spiritual light of truth shall prevail.

Kundalini Energy

The subtle energy of Kundalini merges the internal female and male energies in each of us and leads to the transcendence beyond both. Kundalini is the story of the gods, the god within each of us (Dale, 2009, p. 241). The Mother or womb of God as your creative power is being returned to the throne of each person's awareness (Chuse, 1998).

Kundalini Shakti is an evolutionary energy shrouded in mystery (Morris, Carlson, http://www.kundalinisupportnetwork.com/shaktipat.html) hidden by symbolic codes occult practices and religious dogma. Formerly reserved for high level priesthoods and royalty, this ultimate self-empowerment practice can be developed by an open and willing participant through self-disciplined practice. Yet the Kundalini fire can also be activated by Shaktipat which is hands-on touch that transmits energy through the meridian lines from a person who has experience and demonstrated competence with Kundalini activation.

While Kundalini was activated in me through my own personal meditation practice and mantra chanting, I also later received *Shaktipat* from a guru though I only attended weekly meetings for about a two month period. I felt I was ultimately be responsible for my own spiritual growth. While I have the highest respect for them, I did not want to give away my power to a guru or any other person, as reports at that time were surfacing about misconduct among gurus.

Nevertheless, I learned that "man must become God-like through a life of virtue. He must cultivate his/her spirit through knowledge, practice and discipline in the realization that there is no mediator between him/her and his/her salvation" (Ashby, 2003).

Opening the doors of perception and letting spirit in requires the responsibility to make personal changes in order awaken one's entire being to the energy that animates and connects you to the universe in order that you can live a peaceful and harmonious life.

The arousal of the *Serpent Goddess Kundalini* is the symbol of higher consciousness. She bestows great spiritual gifts and grants wisdom and vision beyond space and time (Arewa, 1998). During this process of spiritual transformation she tosses you around, floods you with emotion, blows down your illusions and cracks apart your material world until you recognize that "your world is an impermanent as autumn leaves" (Valle'e, 2009). Her primeval raw power of transformation is not at all gentle, but fiery and causes trembling as it cuts through obstacles and impediments, shaking things up until balance is achieved and what was earthly becomes celestial (Narby, 1999).

Kundalini acts as a "teacher to the soul." While the initial awakening may have been preceded by a time of grief and despair, the most trying *dark night of the soul* comes at a later stage when there seems to be a withdrawal of divine favor resulting in profound despair (Walters, 2009).

I believe that this period was when I learned that my journey is not under my control, but is directed by some mysterious force that appears to be both inside and outside of me. As my former guru used to say, "You are not the doer of action, you are the seer. Mother will never give you more than you can handle. *It is all Mother's Play of Consciousness*", he would say.

I learned that everything in our existence is a result of or consciousness. You should seek to have *God (Christ in you)* consciousness, and live as if you are never not in *His/Her presence*" (Amen RA Horakhty, 2001).

While individual Kundalini awakening experiences vary from person to person, there are classic signs that an awakening has occurred (Dale, 2011). There are also particular symptoms of pranic (breath) movements, yogic phenomenon, physiological and psychological symptoms, extrasensory and psychic perceptions, as well as mystical states of consciousness which might arise.

Bonnie Greenwell, Ph.D. in an article in *Kundalini Rising*, wrote of symptoms like tingling, heat or cold sensations in or outside the body, energy running through the body, intensified sexual desires, emotional outbursts, mental confusion, increased creativity, seeing flashes of white light, deeper spiritual insights, overwhelming feelings of love, astral projection, soul travel and out of body experiences (OBEs) and other experiences can take place as a result of the awakening of the *Divine Feminine* energy within.

In coping with my own personal signs and symptoms of Kundalini, I was supported and helped most prominently by the writings and counseling from *"Shared Transformation,"* a support group created by El Collie, a person who experienced first-hand the difficulties of KA herself and who became thrust into more severe indications that Kundalini had awakened in her. She experienced more severe symptoms like difficulty swallowing, agitation, insomnia, tremors, drooling, protrusion of the tongue, an inability to remain still, making mask-like faces, spasms of the neck and other body parts (kriyas), a shuffling gait, etc. http://www.elcollie.com/html/Issue9a.html

How I Awakened Kundalini Energy

There are a many ways that the Kundalini Energy can become awakened in a person. My personal KA experience was precipitated by a desire to heal from what I was told was an HIV positive diagnosis from a medical doctor.

I began a search for God, for truth and for healing. I preferred to die from anything other than dying from the stigma of HIV/AIDS. I desperately went from one religious church setting to another, read books about many related topics, sought the help of a Spiritual Guru, attended a Siddha Yoga Ashram, etc...

Yet, it was not until I learned and frequently chanted the mantra, **"Om Namah Shivaya,"** which loosely translates to "I Honor God in Me," or "Om and salutations to that which I am capable of becoming," in meditation did I experience the mystical experience of Kundalini Awakening.

"Nama Sivaya" has power. The mere intonation of these syllables reaps its own reward in salvaging the soul from bondage of the treacherous instinctive mind and the steel bands of a perfected externalized intellect. Nama Sivaya quells the instinct, cuts through the steel bands and turns this intellect within and on itself, to face itself and see its ignorance. Sages declare that mantra is life, that mantra is action, that mantra is love and that the repetition of mantra, japa, bursts forth wisdom from within." --Satguru Sivaya Subramuniyaswami

During meditation that night, I was not sure what had happened to me. All I knew was that from that point my life was changed. I researched intently and intensely for a period of about two years before I came to understand what had happened and what was happening in my life. I realized that I had been spiritually awakened by *The Divine*

Mother God, Serpent Goddess who manifests herself as *Auset, Diana, Maria, Isis, Hecate, Persephone, Sekhmet, Mother-Nature and many other worthy names* that represent archetypes of her all-pervading presence.

The cultivation of Kundalini movement in the body is enhanced when purifying the body is cleansed of toxins and pollutants through physical exercise and eating organic foods (Dale, 2011). As spiritual beings we must also purify our hearts and souls.

Unless and until the body is purified and cleansed of pollution, pesticides, additives in food and other environmental toxics, Kundalini can create havoc one's life and can potentially destabilize the personality, particularly if the spiritual seeker is naïve in their understanding of the major psychological and physical changes involved in spiritual awakening.

Throughout many life times, others' energy patterns can be stored inside our chakra fields. Those patterns came from our ancestry, religion, peer groups and other institutions from which we have absorbed energies.

Purification includes many of the aforementioned activities. Additionally, there are various meditation techniques which can aid in the unhindered flow of Kundalini energy in the body: projection and visualization, bhandas (body locks), mantras (chanted words), kriyas (exercise sets), mudras (hand gestures) and regulation of the four basic instincts (food, sleep, sex and self-preservation).

Shakti Kundalini energy lies coiled 3 and ½ times within the root chakra at the base of the spine to return to the Shiva energy in the seventh chakra which awaiting his lost mate (Dale, 2011, 2009).

After an initiate experiences what has been described by Walters (2000) as "a tiny spark in a great, indescribable, inscrutable force, the unnamed source of all that is, that which animated and powers the universe in overwhelming love," *Mother God* grants wisdom beyond space and time (Arewa, 1998). One gets to see beyond the illusion of limitation and duality, embrace the darkness within and enter the light.

While some energetic systems hold that because of the KA process powers called siddhi become active and grant seemingly godlike magical abilities like the ability to heal, levitation, invisibility and many more which essentially free the initiate from the confines of the physical laws of the universe. Major unresolved psychological issues may cause one to become at risk for constrictions in the mind, body, emotions and psyche brought on by hidden energetic blockages in the body chakra system. Kundalini is unrelenting and presses on until they are cleared.

This troublesome and difficult period brings on bodily sensations and impulses never experienced before. One becomes incredibly sensitive to both pain and pleasure. Even for the most seemingly normal or balanced person there may be episodes of intense alternating between intense bliss and severe pain (Walters, 2000).

There is usually an abrupt shift sense of self and in worldview. Why? Because, all imperfections and weaknesses of the soul must be rooted out. One's diet, harmful addictive habits, destructive patterns of behavior and unresolved conflicts must be healed. Kundalini becomes a "teacher for the soul" and points out these areas that need to be healed.

It is as if from the moment of KA one's life is forever changed. Kundalini can cause havoc in one's life for quite a long time.

Many people seek meaningful psychological help to deal with unconscious motives and desires being pushed to the surface for psychological review and assimilation. One gets the opportunity to integrate denied parts of self into the whole of who they are. Those of you who are self-rejecting need to learn to accept and love yourself. You are worthy and loveable beings. Ego inflation and/or self-deprecation are obstacles to (g)od-realization.

In extreme cases, serious mental and physical damage can be experienced by people if the energy is moving too fast and furiously through the body unleashing unconscious and super conscious material and can create mental chaos for a person. Some people have committed suicide. For persons through whom the energies move too fast or forcefully, prescription drugs might be their only salvation.

Kundalini and the Dangers of Psychotropic Drugs

A person experiencing *spiritual emergency/crisis* should be wary of physicians who want to prescribe neuroleptic anti-depressants, and anti-psychotic drugs like Valium, Librium, Thorazine, Stelazine, Prolixin, Vesprin, Trilafon, Navane, Taractan, Serentil, Orap, Repoise, Compazine, Dartal, Clorazil, Mellaril, Quide, Haldol and Tindal, which could cause life-threatening drug reactions.

While some of the reactions to these drugs are, in fact, identical to Kundalini symptoms, other reactions include and are not limited to strokes, heart poisoning, bone-marrow poisoning, suicide, blood abnormalities, irregular pulse, cerebral edema, endocrine disturbances, catatonia, cardiac arrest, liver damage, petit and grand mal seizures, skin disorders, intestinal paralysis, hypotension, urinary retention, or difficulty urinating, dry mouth, hair loss, impotence, nosebleeds, mood changes, nausea, sensitivity to light, loss of appetite, cramps, convulsions, nightmares, fever, skin rashes, numbness in fingers and toes, ringing in the ears, uncoordinated movements and balance problems, etc.

Bizarre Occurrences

Kundalini can interfere with household electricity. Lights may go dim or flicker. Electrical appliances may break down. Television and radio channels may produce static. Computers or printers might malfunction. Touching other persons can produce an electric shock. Even animals may react differently in the presence of an awakened person, being either magnetized toward or bolting away from them. Kundalini permanently rewires the body-mind to release stored tension. One must release shame, guilt, abuse, denial, and neglect, or any attempt to avoid their *True Nature* in order to better facilitate the movement of the energy of Kundalini that flows throughout the body.

"From that healing moment in time my life changed in ways I did not at the time know were possible."

I ask your indulgence in my presentation of a succinct overview of my experiences without my having to elaborate on such personal and private experiences.

The next day after my KA and from that day forward up to today, I noticed that birds and animals on occasion reacted strangely in my presence. Ravens appeared almost wherever I went: at home, at work, while driving, in the park, while shopping, etc. They frequently swooped in and landed on the ledge of the roof of the building where I lived or in the trees outside my high-rise apartment and cawed ominously. Once they flew in and encircled me in the parking lot outside a mall. Over one hundred of them descended around me once. There were many times when ravens approached me in as few a number as one, two, three, four, five, six, seven, or as many as twenty or a hundred or more. As odd as it may seem, I actually learned to communicate with them, based on the number of caws I heard which I related to the principle of the chakras. If I heard 3 caws, I knew that I should observe the principle to respect myself, etc.

On occasion ravens and hawks or falcons frolicked outside my window or in the air over my head. While visiting my parents in Alabama, I went outside, looked up and there were seven hawks soaring, weaving some pattern among them, high in the air directly overhead. I rushed inside to get my camera phone only to find they had dispersed when I returned. This occurrence was without a doubt a synchronous event. Hawks symbolize emerging higher consciousness. Amazing!

Once I went outside, looked up and was just in time to witness a Hawk snatch a snake from high in a pine tree next door in the neighbor's yard. It was quite a spectacular sight. Had I been a second later, I would not have witnesses it. I wondered what the spiritual significance of seeing such a happening could be.

Throughout the years since my awakening, butterflies, ladybugs, bees and dragonflies also fluttered or buzzed by me regularly and sometimes startled me when they alighted inside my car while waiting at traffic signals. Once I almost had an accident. I recall an incident when I looked out of my window and viewed a fleet of dragonflies which flew back and forth in a rectangular fashion, the length of my apartment for over an hour without resting. I also remember the day a bumblebee alighted outside my 15th floor window nonstop for over an hour without cease.

I want to emphasize that many of these seemingly bizarre behaviors were not just random occurrences. They happened quite frequently as if something wanted to get my attention. I decided to research their spiritual and symbolic significance.

I was led to information about the cyclical stages of spiritual alchemy as well as Native American spirituality. Ravens symbolized the second stage after spiritual transformation and alchemy: awakening, blackening, where an awakened person's life seemingly falls apart in order that they die to their old ways, experience a crucifixion of their former self, resurrect and be reborn anew.

I further learned that of *animal totems* and *spirit guides*. The raven is a powerful animal totem which represents healing, wisdom and protection while working in the void, connection to and communication from ancestors. Raven is the evolutionary form of the prehistoric velociraptor.

Butterflies symbolized transformation. Ladybugs signaled enlightenment. Bees symbolized "working" for the common good, and dragonflies symbolized the breaking down of illusions, which is required when learning of one's true self.

I also learned that some insects are drawn to a person's aura whose Kundalini was awakened, just as bees are drawn to flowers.

Strange animal behavior also startled me. Once, a puppy left its owner and ran clear across a large field in the public park to where I sat talking to a friend and jumped up on my leg and began licking me. I had not called it to me. And yet another time while I jogging, in a crowded park, a boy's pet dog ran across my path only to immediately turn around. It barked ferociously at me while snapping at my lower legs and feet. Yet, acquaintances who owned a seemingly ferocious pit bull on one occasion entered the room where I sat with other people. The dog surveyed the entire room of people, then looked directly at me and calmly walked over to me where I sat between two people on the sofa. It calmly leaned and rested on my leg, as if it had chosen me as a safe place to rest.

As the years unfolded and as I learned more about what was happening to me, I began to appreciate the new awareness that I was gaining. I learned to recognize the spiritual significance of certain animals and insects that appeared in my environment. I learned of shamanism and considered that perhaps I was an urban shaman in training.

One day I was sitting on bleachers in the park writing in my journal. I had just written the last word of thanks to God for the birds and the bees when all of a sudden two birds flew right by my head while a large bumblebee simultaneously landed on my backpack that was positioned right next to me.

Synchronous and bizarre events became commonplace. I could be thinking of a person and suddenly they would appear around the next corner or call me over the telephone. I seemed to have perceived premonitions of things to come. An intuitive flash would come to my mind, and the sun would part the clouds and shine on my ideas.

I had a most amazing day as a Pre-K Lead teacher. The children and I had come in from the playground and were just getting seated on the carpet for storytime. We were singing and doing finger plays. Oh, how I miss those days. All of a sudden, since the back door to the classroom had been left open to allow heat from the summer sun to get in to cut the chill of the too-cold air conditioner, a black butterfly flew in. It fluttered and circled over the children. They gasped and smiled and reached for the butterfly. All of a sudden it swooped down and landed directly on my chest right over my high-heart. I could hardly believe it as I leaned back in astonishment. Then, it flew up, circled over the children again and came back and landed in that exact same spot on my heart. Then it flew up, up and away, back out the back door. I looked at my co-teacher and we both smiled and shrugged our shoulders. The awesome magnificence of the black butterfly graced me with its presence, and confirmed what I had already known, that I was indeed an urban shaman in training. I could not help remembering the awesome song called Black Butterfly sung by the beautiful and talented Black Butterfly herself, Deniece Williams. Here her sing of the wisdom of the Black Butterfly at: https://www.youtube.com/watch?v=60Clm6lUzjM. I went home that day and cried, because I was so profoundly moved and grateful by the experience of having a Black Butterfly land on me, twice in one day.

I later learned of Richard Moss, M.D. just by chance. He had written a book called The Black Butterfly: An Invitation to Radical Aliveness, which I bought and read. In it, among many other things, confirmed my awareness that diseases are a blessing and grant opportunities for spiritual growth.

I also experienced long periods of depression and suicidal ideation, as well as periods of ecstatic joy and bliss. At times, I slipped into licentious behaviors and experienced parts of my being that I would never have thought possible. I believe that I was experiencing the *dark night of the soul* which seemed to be unending. I felt abandoned by God for several years. I prayed. I begged God to relieve me of the pain I was experiencing. Nothing I chose to do worked well for me. I continued to pray fervently for it to end and for my life to get better, but to no avail. I later realized that I had become what I had judged as deplorable in others, namely an alcohol abuser and an illegal drug user. I am so happy to have self-healed from self-destructive behaviors. You can too.

Kundalini, Holy Spirit, The Great Mother, Divine Feminine, once awakened, breaks down a person's illusions and annihilates the ego, or sense of separateness one feels from others and God. Sometimes it is necessary to become that which you think you hate in order that you assimilate the shadow side of yourself, making transformation extremely difficult at times.

She also bestows grace, awakens truth and grants the experience of different realities.

I now see 11s frequently, either, multiples, numbers adding up to 11 or some derivation thereof: 111, 2:11, 7:11, etc., some sort of communication code. I see them on clocks, car tags, home addresses, billboards, phone numbers, and store receipts frequently. How is it that just when I decide to look up I see 12:34 on the clock, or when I pass the microwave that I had set for 60 seconds, I just so happen to look up at just the right time to see 11 seconds left? Why would I repeatedly wake up and see 3:33 or 4:44 on the clock?

While sleeping or drifting to sleep, or waking up in the middle of the night, I had frequent out-of-body experiences (OBEs). I read many books on the subjects of soul travel, astral projection and OBEs. I studied techniques for facilitating their occurrence. When I finally overcame the fear of leaving my body, I visited other worlds nightly assisted by beings that I believe to be *"Star People,"* a term I prefer to extraterrestrial, whose loving presence I could only sense and feel, but who I could not see. I chose to not see, except for one time in particular, because I thought I would become overly frightened which would likely prevent me from future explorations. Communication between us was telepathic.

It is said that when one's Kundalini is awakened, s/he can be seen from deep in space.

Out-Of-Body Experiences (OBEs)

A most memorable OBE was when a heavenly Black male Star-Being assisted me on a tour of what appeared to be a world of swirling colors of purple and lavender. His skin was dark and vibrant. His hair was wooly and his eyes blazed like the sun. The experience was breathtaking.

The most memorable OBE to date was when I had an open 3rd eye experience. I lay down, closed my eyes and began to see colors and shapes behind closed eyes. Suddenly, was pulled through a tunnel at incredible speed. I emerged in the cosmos. I flew as if assisted by beings that were glad to have me there. They were happy to have a person who let go of fear in order that they could show me the wonders of the universe. I saw infinite galaxies in the distance as I hurtled through space. It was the most exhilarating experience to date. The experience went on for so long. I felt so far away from my body on the bed that I began to fear being able to return to it. The instant I had that thought of fear, I began the backwards travel back into my body that lay on the bed. I lay there vibrating back down into my body for almost a minute. I got up and paced my apartment absolutely amazed, invigorated and exhilarated by what I had just experienced.

I even composed original poetry and made journal entries detailing what I could remember of my night-time voyages. One such poem was:

Beyond the Body

> They were here last night
> Carried me for another ride
> Tickled my feet, supported my shoulders, stroked my hair
> At incredible speed we flew through the air
> Longed and wished to be whisked away
> Hued and breathed, relaxed and prayed
> Let the physical body go
> No fear to be had
> Then came the vibes
> Gave in to the flow
> Up and away
> Dimensions unknown

A cosmic adventure one more time
Look forward to the next
What a thrilling ride
Focus on love, worlds beyond
Worlds within
Thank God for the fun

~Damian Laster

There were also mornings when I woke up and heard incredible symphonies and/or beautiful poetry in my head which most certainly were not my own creations; beautiful symphonic orchestrations and angelic choral renderings.

Each experience ended with me traveling in reverse direction and re-emerging into my body and vibrating and/or pulsing back down into my physical vessel. This was a literal physical sensation. It was as if my consciousness and or astral body had to readjust now that it was back inside my physical body. There were frequent Kundalini internal pulsations and vibrations.

I had also regularly made nightly contact with what I refer to as *Star People*. I requested and received what I term "vibrational healing" from the Arcturians/Medical Assistance Program (MAP Teams). I learned of them in Dr. Joshua Stones "Ascension Manual." The MAP teams came when requested and used some sort of rod-like instrument, which was place on areas of my body. It vibrated those areas back to health. The physical sensation was one of raising the frequency of vibration of internal organs.

While in the dream state, I learned of my *"multidimensional self"* and came to know that I exist in many worlds as a different version of myself while here in this 3rd dimension of earth existence. I counted 12 {Me(s)}. Some of those worlds were verisimilar to this one. Some

149

of the people I encountered are in those worlds (parents, friends, environments) though not all of them. Bizarre? Yes. I would not feign such a story. I noticed patterns and was able to literally count 12. I later learned that we have 12 soul extensions.

Many times I questioned my own sanity and feared sharing my experiences with others. Fortunately my mother listened and did her best to understand what I was revealing. She read many of the books I shared with her so that she would better understand and be able to support my transformation.

I was a voracious reader of all things metaphysical. I accepted the intuitive flashes that frequently occurred.

I also required periods of rest and relaxation whenever Kundalini caused intense energetic surges throughout my body. Without warning intense lethargy could overcome me out of nowhere. Lying down and relaxing or letting go of the body as well as letting go of any doubts and fears helped relieve KA symptoms. This allowed the energy to move less obstructed which relieved internal pressure. I drank copious amounts of water.

I also felt as if being rewired from the inside. I refer to it as an "oval of energy" or "egg of energy" in an area of the body that could be felt as if reorganizing something internal, perhaps altering or activating my DNA.

My research led me to a book called Kundalini Rising. In it, one experience detailed a woman named *Whitehawk* who spoke of Kundalini leading her to profound liberation in which she relinquished her need for control in favor of absolute trust and surrender to the strangeness that becomes part and parcel of life when Kundalini takes the reins.

She too had had OBEs, experiences in other realms with beings in nonphysical realms. She said Kundalini had "stretched her beyond previous limits into entirely new octaves of existence." She corresponded with the beings from the Pleiades in other worlds, higher dimensions, or in traveling craft. "Walls, objects, even the air itself seemed alive with their energetic essence...," she wrote.

Many of my OBE and astral experiences seemed to be some sort of *initiation process* where I was required to overcome fear(s). I had to traverse seemingly impossible terrains or staircases, breathe under water, walk through fire, or through walls, or fly, sometimes at incredible speeds hurtling through the sky or cosmos. Whenever I was overcome with fear I would immediately travel back into my body and wake up and know that I had failed the test. Other times, while lucid, I recognized that I was being tested. I released all fear and launched into the task without fear and was amazed at just how easy it was for me to perform a seemingly impossible task. Other times I became conscious and lucid while in the dream state and was able to direct the action at the speed of thought. I learned that the challenge was to become aware (conscious) even while asleep. I had to learn that there was nothing to fear but fear itself. Whenever I did that, transcending any situation or environment was incredibly easy.

I read experiences of other people too many to discuss here.

Imagine my surprise when I learned Shurlene and Earlene Carr, two African American sisters called, "The UFO TWINS," who wrote a book, *"From the Motherland to the Mothership"* detailing their interaction with extraterrestrials from other worlds. They confirmed my experiences of traveling to distant planets. I listened to several of their Blog-Talk Radio interviews too. I literally cried when similarities were revealed between their experiences and mine. Hear them for yourself. http://www.blogtalkradio.com/isiswisdom/2011/05/15/saturday-night-exclusive-interview-with-ufo-twins.

The UFO Twins and I, had been led to read many of the same books, among them *Conversations with God, You Can Heal Your Life, The Sirius Mystery, and The Celestine Prophecy*. We had read others works more related to our own race and ethnicity by authors like Dr. Yosef A. A. ben-Jochannan, Dr. John Henry Clarke, W.E.B. Dubois, Richard King and others who taught us that we are gods and instilled cultural pride in us. They taught us facts about ancestry and about ourselves and our history, which we were denied learning in the traditional education system here in the United States public school system. We listened to metaphysical master teachers like Dr. Delbert Blair, Dr. Phil Valentine, and Brother Bobby Hemmit, Dr. Jewel Pookrum, MD, and many others. We are forever grateful to them.

Spiritual Focus

One's spiritual focus must contribute to an expansion of consciousness and the deepening of one's life and contribution to life. http://biologyofkundalini.com/article. php?story=KundaliniPracticeSkillsList&mode=print.

Grounding, relaxation, toning, various breathing techniques, raw diet, cold showers, foot baths, sun and rock meditation, mindfulness, affirmations and visualization are all ways help oneself manage changes taking place within an awakened body.

My former guru frequently said, *"You are not the doer of action. You are the seer. It is all Mother's Play of Consciousness. And, Mother will never give you more than you can handle." --Chris Chambers*

The stronger the Shakti energy in a person, they are more likely to experience mysterious forms of the cosmic play of consciousness.

The Kundalini manifestations are not proof that a person is falling apart: they are signs of inner growth and change. This process unfolds in its own way and at its own pace. http://www.elcollie.com/html/Issue9a.html

Cindi Dale (2011) shared that managing KA signs and symptoms can be affected by:

~resolving childhood problems,

~releasing energies that are not your own,

~setting energetic boundaries,

~activating intuitive spiritual gifts,

~connecting to the Divine,

~seeking spiritual guidance and protection,

~eliminating energetic bindings, curses and entity attachments,

~integrating soul fragments,

~setting energetic boundaries,

~embracing limits,

~and making healthy lifestyle choices can allow for a more supportive and comfortable Kundalini Awakening.

While the more order we reflect in our life the healthier we are, healing does not come from us. It comes from the "pure awareness" of God. It is not a vibration but from the source of vibration, and potential order and energy of every form (Kinslow, 2008). Procedures do not heal. Thoughts do not heal. Awareness does the healing.

In fact, it was when I had "slipped beyond thought and just existed" in the gap between thoughts, that Mother God granted me the grace of healing and so much more.

> *"The fire is lit. You are fulfilled, and this fulfillment gives you peace."*
>
> *--Patricia Jepsen Chuse*

Wisdom of the Ancestors

The term "subtle energies" of Kundalini is not new, the idea of subtle energies is embedded in human history, as our ancestors developed methods and systems to work with healing energies of the cosmos within ourselves. Whether Hindu, Tibetan, Mayan, Cherokee, Incan, Christian, Egyptian, African, or Jewish, etc., all systems agree that the human body is really a universe composed of energy bodies--swirling vortices of light that literally transform sensory energy to spiritual energy, and vice versa (Dale, 2009).

And while there was a schism between Western and Eastern Medicine, practitioners and patients noticed that the two approaches enhanced one another. Western Medicine is allopathic and mechanistic and seeks to alleviate symptoms through scientifically documented methods. Eastern medicine, on the other hand, is devoted to holistic health care which treats the total person--mind, body and spirit.

With the knowledge that diseases are energetic and that energetic imbalances ensue as a result of consciousness, health can be restored and established by balancing one's energies using an integrative care approach.

Mother God's awakening in me allowed me to gain this knowledge intuitively but the most exciting studies are now being done using leading edge equipment, physics and processes in laboratories, clinics, institutes and universities around the world where history meets research to yield proof and substantiate the existence of subtle energy structures in the body that are intricately linked to the chakra system (Dale, 2009).

Studies using super-conducting quantum interference devices which perceive electromagnetic energies beyond the bounds of the body, as well as processes that embeds human intention onto a simple electrical device show the effects of thought on physicality. While these subtle energies operate by different rules than do measurable energies can completely ignore time and space, change form at will and occupy many places at once. (Dale, 2009)

Respected researcher, physicist and expert on subtle energy, Dr. William Tiller's model shows that subtle energies flow downward from the highest, "the Divine", providing a template for the level below. There was once a single consciousness that unified everything within which was Shiva (Infinite Supreme Consciousness) and *Shakti (Eternal Supreme Consciousness). Shiva* represents time and *Shakti* represents space. These two beings separated, creating a distinction between matter and consciousness within the universe. Within people this energy lies dormant and coiled within the base of the spine.

When Kundalini is awakened the masculine (electrical) and feminine (magnetic) energies within the person frees him/her from the confines of the physical body. Innate powers—magical and mystical abilities--awaken. That describes exactly what happened to me. *"It was as if I had slipped beyond time and just existed" (Horakhty, 2001).*

Moreover, the soul is freed from the wheel of life that forces reincarnation. When balance and blending of both energies is achieved there is harmony and within harmony, healing.

From HIV to Kundalini Awakening the Divine Feminine Within

There came a time when I also shared with others my research and revelations regarding the HIV debacle. They read my manuscript, *"The Rainbow Warrior: Healing HIV through Chakra Awareness"* and initially thought I was deluded and confused.

155

Six years after I completed that previous manuscript, a friend sent me a link to an article written by Djhuty Maat RA, a world renowned nutritionist; a man who like me had changed made an ancient African spiritual name for himself just as I had, my spiritual name being Kabir Amen RA Horakhty. His article http://www.starseeds.net/group/glbtstarseeds/forum/topics/h-i-v-aids-debunked {no longer available on dherbs.com} essentially said the same things that I had been saying for years. He pointed out facts delineated earlier in this book. He wrote a comprehensive overview of the HIV debacle and crisis and debunked it. I will forever respect his courage to tell the truth about HIV/AIDS.

Other nutritionists and classical virologists began to publish information questioning conventional HIV/AIDS including but not limited to Dr. Phil Valentine, Dr. Jewell Pookrum, M.D., Dr. Scott Whitaker, ND, Jose Fleming, CN, MH and Dr. Llaila Africa. They arrived at the same conclusions that I had gained from the personal experience of being impacted by an HIV positive diagnosis, researching the crises and removing myself from that paradigm. They, like I, were diligently working to expose deception and raise public awareness in an effort to save lives.

Many friends and associates who had received an HIV positive diagnosis and who experienced debilitating direct effects of their toxic drug prescriptions thanked me for providing views of which they were not familiar. They are no longer taking them and are healthy once again.

I have received many emails from people around the world who have shared articles I wrote with their friends and loved ones. One such article titled *"Let HIV Set You Free,"* published in 2006. http://aras.ab.ca/articles/popular/200607-Laster.html

While some people have not been able to accept my revelations as truth, generally those who have experienced conventional HIV therapies are glad to consider a new approach since the ones they used created horrible effects like nausea, vomiting, mental confusion, numbness in the fingers and toes (peripheral neuropathy), etc.

Many personal friends and associates who persisted in their prescribed toxic drug regimens for an HIV positive diagnosis have passed. They succumbed to fear and toxic drugs.

But for me, the threat of death from an HIV positive diagnosis propelled the evolution of my conscious awareness of God in me, as me. According to Samael Aun Weor, *"the progress, development and evolution in Kundalini is very slow and difficult, disciples must have a system of purification and sanctification. They must make a list of their defects and amend them orderly and methodically to allow the Inner Christ to flourish.*

HIV/Kundalini Reflections and Lessons Learned

Socrates said, "The unexamined life is not worth living." The only true wisdom is in knowing that you know nothing." (Kinslow, 2008)

As the cycles of spiritual and alchemical transformation in my life unfold, I am learning to honor others, to respect myself, to love unconditionally, to surrender personal will to Divine Will, to seek only the truth, to release anger, be compassionate, forgive self and others and to live in the present moment of awareness while endeavoring to recognize the oneness of all life.

"They slept until the black raven, blithe hearted proclaimed the joy of heaven.--Beowulf http://www.druidry.org/obod/lore/animal/raven.html

In an instant, the serpent *Goddess Kundalini* energy can rise up the spine of a person and grant wisdom beyond space and time, granting special psychic abilities called siddhis. Among these gifted precognition, teleportation (OBEs), remote viewing, clairvoyance, clairaudience and clairsentience, as well as the ability to see into and travel to the outer realms and other dimensions to experience the entities and environments there.

For some people, the energy surge of Kundalini is intense and can lead to more dramatic behaviors and physical, emotional and mental challenges. Grounding and breathing techniques, prayer, relaxation and eating a raw food diet can help ease the effects of Kundalini.

Kundalini support groups, whether online or in a physical setting also provide immense support especial for those who have been misdiagnosed as schizophrenic.

As you begin to understand what is happening in your life as a result of KA your sense of separateness from others and from God is realized through the inevitable process of ego annihilation. You get the opportunity to heal past traumas and unresolved psychological issues to help restore energetic balance to your body.

I have contended that there has been a fraudulent imposition on the public who have allowed themselves to be brainwashed about HIV. *Mother Goddess Kundalini* has revealed through the KA experience that health comes from within.

You can align yourself with healing energies and restore health to your body whether you experience difficulties assimilating the divine energies awakened by Kundalini or physical symptoms of illness related to fear, shame and guilt from receiving an HIV+ diagnosis or any other dis-ease with self.

Detoxifying and purifying your body, meditation, relaxation, chanting mantras can help awaken the *Holy Spirit* within you. Healing wounds through forgiveness, obtaining loving support, affirming all-good in your life, utilizing creative visualization, eating a proper diet and raising the overall frequency of your body can help facilitate healing from any illness.

I agree with Neale Donald Walsh who said that *"we are waking up to our true gifts--and stewarding the emergence of a new era. We're evolving a new form of masculinity--one fused with integrity, authenticity, generosity and virtue. And we're living more purposefully and finding ways to serve a cause greater than ourselves. It is not an easy path. We're learning as we go--transforming our past, expressing our inner strengths in new ways. We're learning to lead boldly without dominating, feel fully and freely, and use our power to protect instead of destroy. And we have further to go--both for the sake of our liberation and the world's."* http://www.thegetalifetimes.com/?p=494

I attribute this new awareness to the energy of *Mother Goddess Kundalini. Holy Spirit* re-awakening in the consciousness of humanity.

Gonna tell a story morning glory all about the serpentine fire." Earth Wind and Fire

Her awakening in me inspired this poem:

"Goddess Energy"

What is this movement that's stirring in me?
Something's awakened. What can it be?
Lying or standing or sitting in place
My legs, my stomach, my chest, my face.
Something has happened to ignite such a spark.
If feels like a pulse from deep in my heart.
I know it as separate from the flow of my blood.
It whirls. It fidgets. It really feels good.

Balancing my energy, regenerating my cells,
Pulling and tugging restoring me well.
I guess I AM chosen as all of us are,
If we would but notice and be who we are.
No need to pretend that I'm something I'm not,
For God is expressing and that is my lot.
Relax, Relate, Release, and Be Free.
Acknowledge my uniqueness, to live and to be.
All that I am whether different or same,
Loving myself is the name of the game.
Only then can I love others as well,
Forgiving them and listening to the stories they tell.
I've researched and figured it out to be
The loving force of Goddess Energy
The Serpent is aroused------ Kundalini!

Original Poetry by Damian Q. Laster
aka Kabir Horakhty

Perhaps the awakening of my Kundalini was a call to world service, a personal mission bigger than me. And while I recognize the oneness of all life, I also realize that I am not here to fit in. I am a systems buster available for altering systems of consciousness. I am a member of the Renegade Family of Light and am here to be different, to totally and completely upset status quo reality. Everything I thought was wrong with me is exactly what was right with me and perfect for the realization of my awesome magnificence. And as I continue on the continual cycle of spiritual transformation of birth, growth, death and return, I will gain experience of God in me, as me.

"You plotted evil against me, but God turned it into good in order to preserve the lives of many people..." (Gen. 50:20). Hence, a merging of opposites at the heart chakra, and ascension into higher levels of conscious awareness, from *HIV to Kundalini: Awakening the Divine Feminine Within.*

Healing Emotional Pain

> *"Time does not heal everything…It just teaches us how to live with pain."*

How do you deal with the emotional pain of an HIV+ diagnosis even after learning that the whole thing is a farce and people think you are crazy for even thinking that? What I do is patiently wait for worldwide awakening, forgive myself for all the years of running away from myself and for not having loved myself more than I did. Folks tell addicts to pray the Serenity Prayer. I will not lie and not say that every time I pray that prayer I wonder about the "…wisdom to know the difference" part. "Should I do something or should I do nothing?"

I choose to do! To the best of my ability and within the scope of my will, I turn rage into radiance by taking action. I no longer run away from me. I cannot run away from the world as it is any longer.

I refuse to run away from my truth or live a lie.

My view about the perspective of people who spew hatred for homosexuals and slander them at every opportunity is that even the Diagnostic and Statistical Manual was oppressive toward homosexuals up until 1972. Homosexual persons were labeled as abnormal. Homosexuality was considered a mental disorder. I am surprised that anyone would even give that resource relevance to describe homosexuality.

Further, blaming white supremacist notions for homosexuality is misguided, though in part might be valid in certain contexts. Yet, no one can make a person who is not homosexual become homosexual. There are however those who have been confused about who they are as men and women. They are not homosexuals. They are confused, or at best, are undecided. All LGBT members are born the way God intended. Rape during slavery did not cause Black men to become homosexual. Most rapist and molesters are heterosexual.

Homosexuality is not something to be cured. It is a soul expression to be experienced in this particular lifetime. A person makes a soul contract prior to incarnating to experience this lifetime in this dimension as a homosexual. Stop blaming homosexuality on Europeans. Homosexuals have more of a balance of masculine and feminine energies and therefore more creative ability. In African tribes, homosexuality was never an issue to be scoffed at. Homosexuals were considered the two-spirited people of the tribe, the gatekeepers who guarded the gates between the world of spirit and the physical world. Homosexuals served as healers and shamans of the tribe.

Be careful when entertaining the views of narcissistic people who fear homosexuality. Never let anyone convince you that you are a mental disorder. So-called conscious people who claim that you are disdainful are not conscious at all.

Addiction

As an avid HIV dissenter and truth-teller and advocate for medical and scientific justice as a community outreach activist, I do my part to be the change I want to see in the world. Meanwhile, I channel the energies of worry, doubt, fear, anger and sadness by channeling energies into areas that will enhance my being-ness in the world, rather than seek it in a bottle of alcohol like I did for many years. I am learning to sit content in my emotional pain and know that everything is alright as it is. I accept that I can live with emotional-pain as a pathway to peace. Pain is a part of life. Pain lets us know that we are alive.

I take action to expose the atrocities of HIV antibody testing. I use what I learned about self-healing to help others who are interested in learning about their spiritual selves and the gift of illnesses, including the awareness that body parts and organs perform physical and spiritually significant symbolic functions for us. Eyes help us see the past, present and future clearly. Ears represent the capacity for hearing the truth. The throat is the center of expression. The heart is the center of love. Arms hold life's experiences. Our stomach digests our ideas. Legs carry us through life, and so on. Through chakra awareness I allow my illnesses to teach me more about myself; mainly that I have the potential to love more, forgive more, release more, have more compassion and stand up for myself.

Addictions showed me that I did not know how to love myself fully. I was running away in fear from myself and from life as it is. I now know that I can use my illnesses as a roadmap to recovery. We transcend addiction(s) when we choose to love ourselves fully, knowing that we are safe, loving and loveable. We can choose to see the world as friendly.

As far as transcending the stigma of HIV and having to deal with being ostracized, I allow life to unfold as it is and wisely let the chips fall where they may. And then I pray:

God-Self,

Grant me the serenity to accept the things I cannot change; the gumption to change the things I cannot accept; courage to change the things I can; and the wisdom to know the difference.

Living one day at a time; Enjoying one moment at a time;

Accepting hardships as the pathway to peace;

Taking this world as it is, not as I would have it;

Trusting that all things will be made right when I surrender to divine will;

That I may be reasonably happy in this illusion.

Amen RA

Anger

For many years, I did not realize that my self-destructive behaviors stemmed from the *anger* that I had felt for far too long after receiving an HIV+ diagnosis. You would think that when I learned that HIV is a farce and I no longer needed to take the prescribed toxic drugs or experience their harmful "direct-effects," that I would have been relieved and overjoyed. Well, I was, but only for a very brief period.

First, I had to adjust to the shocking news from my diligent research. I was led to information about who all the key players are/were in the creating the lies and deceptions about HIV. As mentioned in the introduction to this book, I would not name names. (Those names are readily available through research.) I examined the chronology of events. I could see for myself the continuing deception on tell-lie-vision. I also learned that the voice of HIV dissent was being squelched by big media.

I had literally gone into the belly of the beast and attempted to expose the issue but was met with mean-spirited people who maligned me. One guy who headed a group sponsored by AID Atlanta for Black men, A Deeper Love, in the late 1990s literally told me that his group was not the place to discuss such an issue. Many years later, another group, also sponsored by AID Atlanta, housed in a Jewish Temple complex, was kind enough to allow me to share my views at an offshoot organization they had created for people like me called Evolution Project at a different location across town. The coordinator at AID Atlanta would not talk directly with me, but he referred me to the guy who headed the Evolution Project. I actually grew to respect that guy. He listened seemingly intently to me and ostensibly showed concern.

I participated in two events there, one that I created, "The Metaphysics of Self-Healing". I used hands on experiences to teach awareness and knowledge of the chakras and self-healing principles. I had decided to gently lead the groups' members into knowledge about HIV dissent, but never got to that part due to interruption by an AID Atlanta employee who came in late and vilified me in front of everybody there.

It had taken so much courage to go into a group like that to share my truth. I had been assured that it was a safe place. I wanted to be liked by all the people there. I wondered if the guy who came in late was a "plant" and intended to do just what he did, throw me off, shock me and then scare me away. He vilified me, called me crazy, and questioned my motives. He diminished my educational background and qualifications, saying that my doctorate degree in metaphysics was not a respected science, etc. The guy who headed that program had to apologize to me in front of all the members who had witnessed the assault on my character.

I was so shocked by his seemingly impromptu performance that I did not realize that I was being given an opportunity to pass the test; a test to truly live by the principle of the 3rd chakra; to respect yourself. I had temporarily forgotten that the outer world reflects the inner world. My anger was being reflected back to me by the accusatory AID Atlanta employee. For all intents and purposes, in my role as a teacher and healer at the event, I chose to allow a *psychic vampire* to drain my *solar plexus energy* and halt my program. Had I remained fully present in that moment of awareness, I would have recognized that I was under a *psychic attack*. I could have told everybody that people like him come into and go out of our lives. They come to test our will. They come to steal our joy, thwart our plans, and upset our program. They are vampires of energy. I could have talked about the color yellow and how one could pulse and send energy from the solar plexus, or green love energy from the heart chakra, or red from the root chakra to **create** outcomes of our choosing, rather than allow others to manipulate our creations.

That night, I sat at home and got angry at not having passed the test. I chose to go to the liquor store. I *swallowed by anger* instead of expressing my feelings. I depressed my feelings instead of expressing them in the moment.

I had not fully healed myself of the anger I had felt for many years. I had not freed myself from the self-destructive behavior of addiction at that time.

Incidentally, to make up for the employee's behavior, I assume, I was subsequently invited again to AID Atlanta Evolution Project. I would get another opportunity to speak to a larger group of Black homosexual men, the very people I was intending to help, young Black men who were diagnosed HIV+. I would share my story and research. The "Ask the Experts" panel would include a medical doctor, a religious representative and me, a representative of spiritual knowledge. That day, the medical doctor could not be present but the religious guy and I were there. Both of us shared our story. He spoke about how he had thought that he was going to die while lying in a hospital bed. He called on Jesus, who he claimed came to save him. He spoke about faith in Jesus. He said, he knew Jesus would save him.

I, on the other hand, spoke about the joys of having transcended the lie of HIV after awakening to the truth. I spoke about how glad I was that I had stopped taking the poisonous drugs. I spoke about all the metaphysical things I learned and about my own spiritual growth that took place as a result of the threat of death from HIV. I spoke about all the things I learned about the body-mind-soul-spirit connection. You get the picture.

I had instantly recognized the religious panel member when I walked in. We had chat on a popular social networking site for homosexual men a few years prior. I could see when viewing his photos that he was likely taking ARVS. I could see that his face looked caved-in. His skin was darkened. He looked ravaged by HIV drugs, almost as if life energy was being drained from his body. He looked like he was holding on for dear life. At the event, he wore a neat haircut, wore baggier clothes and smiled a lot, but I was not at all physically attracted to his appearance even back when I first encountered him on the social site. He exuded no sexual energy.

Immediately after the panel discussion ended, I went over to him, gave him my phone number and asked him to call me so we could get together and talk. I wanted to share more information with him. I gave him my number. He said he would call. I noticed how several of the AID Atlanta employees looked on while I was talking with him. Immediately afterwards when I walked away, they swarmed over to him. Needless to say, he never called me. About 6 months or so to a year later, I learned that he had died. I wished that I could have done more to help him save himself because Jesus had, in fact not come to save him.

The loving universe had brought us together and for me to give him an opportunity to learn the truth about HIV but he refused what he had been asking for. I was going to share information with him that would give him an opportunity to save himself, but he listened to AID Atlanta employees. You see what happened.

I refer to all Black HIV activists who are US Government Grant Writers and Receivers as "Smiling-Negroes". They "cheese and grin" for the cameras to have their photos snapped, receive accolades, and are praised as do-gooders, then they go out into communities and urge Black men women and children to that the test. They know not what they are doing, and are mere minions for their masters who use them to route their own people into the HIV death campaign. Those agents are the very people I wanted to reach, and I did. But I do not think that they listened to me. I used to funnel HIV dissent resources (book titles, videos, journal articles, etc.) through the email to each of them for almost a year until some of them changed their email address. I never heard back, not even one time, from any of them.

Years later I called to speak with the guy who had headed the group and who had invited me to attend. I wanted to know how he was doing and how the group members were doing. I learned that he was no longer employed there. I wondered if he had come to his senses and resigned from AID Atlanta. If he had resigned, I know it must have been hard to leave. Perhaps be had been fired. All I know for certain is that the young men who were members of the *Evolution Project* were required to be between the ages of 18 and 28. They were so full of enthusiasm, much of which I attributed to his presence and personality. One member told me that he was like a father to all of them. The project heads at AID Atlanta are paid handsomely. Leaving a job like that where they are praised for doing what they do in the community must initially seem like a great job to have. I know that many of them are only doing what they believe to be best for the community. But, when exposed to the truth, any conscientious person would immediately resign and become a person like I am who exposes the truth about HIV.

I have met at least 2 other people who worked in other states who quit that kind of job when they learned the truth about HIV. I admire and respect them. Popular television shows for homosexual Black men almost always had a likeable character who played the role of the Black homosexual HIV activist. I wondered who funded those shows.

Nevertheless, I was often rejected by the very people I was trying to help not have to fall into all the traps that I had fallen into. I wanted to keep them from living through the hell that I lived through. I wrote this book mostly for them.

I tried to tell them that somebody tried to murder me; that the whole thing was one big lie. Few heeded my warning.

The disappointment and anger I felt at times was overbearing. Surely there was nothing more sinister in the world than somebody benefitting from having me and others think that we are contaminated and potential sexual contaminants. Somebody was responsible for creating conditions for us to be ostracized, stigmatized and marginalized. Somebody was responsible for creating so much fear that people were jailed for sexual activity.

The most devastating and debilitating fear for me was thinking that I was an abomination to God and that I was being punished for being me. Those feelings led to new levels of intense sadness, anger, isolation. I used alcohol and illegal drugs to numb the pain and escape the rejection I was experiencing from seemingly everybody I encountered.

If that wasn't enough already, I became even angrier after experiencing how difficult it was to get over my "fears" and muster the courage to share my story with others via the internet. I decided to post my works, *Metaphysician, Heal Thyself* and, *From HIV to Kundalini: Awakening the Divine Feminine Within*. I had already condensed my first book to an article and was published by David Crowe, on Alberta Reappraising AIDS Society http://aras.ab.ca/articles/popular/200607-Laster.html. I am forever grateful to him for giving me my first outlet to share my experiences within a forum of HIV dissenters where I posted my article *Let HIV Set You Free*. It was being well-received wherever I posted it on the internet.

I decided that I could handle the rejection and the name-calling that would accompany being a whistleblower and a truth-teller. The message was too important to hang my head and walk away from the opportunity to raise awareness and possibly help others save themselves from the shame, pain, and HIV stigma, and from being ostracized after receiving a so-called HIV+ diagnosis.

Later, I had to deal with the feelings of anger that arose when I realized that there appeared to be little I could do to wake people up about the HIV deception and bring about a swift end to the nightmare that I and many others were living. I realized that I was an awakened person in an un-awakened world. Even though I had healed my body, I allowed self-destructive behaviors to fragment my soul. I had turned all that anger inwardly and it was being expressed outwardly each time I chose to give in to self-loathing.

I share with you that I learned to ex-press rather than de-press. I chose to talk about how I was feeling rather than run away in fear. I chose and still choose to let the chips fall where they may when dealing with vehement opposition. I learned to stand my ground and repel energy vampires. I now choose ME. I do not worry about what other people think of me. I choose to take action.

I consciously choose to turn anger into action and experience appreciation and encouragement from many people who thank me for doing what I do. I expose the truth of the HIV deception and strive to be a living example of what I teach. As a result, I do not feel so bad and I no longer drink alcohol or use illegal drugs. I hope you choose to do the same for yourself and for the world. *Turn rage into radiance!*

Isolation

We have discussed transforming and transcending emotional pain. Despite feelings of anger, sadness and frustration of receiving an HIV+ diagnosis, you are learning to move beyond that into living a life filled with joy. You learned that you can express rather than depress your feelings. You also learned how taking action and making the decision to speak your truth about the farce of the HIV debacle and crisis can transform the energy of anger from rage into radiance. You have learned the importance of freeing yourself from self-destructive behaviors.

Now, let us talk about feelings of isolation. Respectfully, a man once asked me, "How do you deal with the emotional pain of not being able to find a partner after you have received an HIV positive diagnosis?" My immediate reaction was to withdraw, cringe, become tearful and lower my head. I had not been in a love/romantic relationship since two years prior to foolishly taking a meaningless test and receiving an HIV+ diagnosis. I was not an *awakened* person at that time. I contemplated how best to answer his question. It stirred all kinds of negative emotions that could have led to deep emotional pain and consequently to emotional imbalance

Living through the HIV crisis led me to isolate myself from others. Whether others withdrew form me or whether I decided to withdraw from them, the result was that I was left isolated. Talking with un-awakened people about spiritual matters had only made me an outcast. Living in a world that was largely un-awakened to spiritual matters made me an outcast. Talking to un-awakened people about the farce of HIV and unethical HIV antibody testing procedures and scientific mumbo-jumbo that was designed to confuse and kill, only made me feel more and more isolated as the years went by. In fact, the whole HIV lexicon (language) of HIV limited people's ability to think rationally and critically about the issue. Words and phrases like HIV+ or HIV-, know your status, viral load, t-cell count, cd-4 count, full blown aids, "the virus," etc. lulled many into and away from their ability for critical thinking.

You have an opportunity awaken and free yourself from the whole paradigm.

The fear associated with receiving an HIV+ diagnosis is real for many people, especially when they allow themselves to be conditioned, manipulated and mind-controlled into fearing sex, fearing self and fearing other people.

Where does that leave a person who receives an HIV + diagnosis? Is it possible to love and be loved in intimate relationships? The answer, a resounding, "Yes"! How? Transform feelings of isolation. Transcend isolation with courage to speak truth to would-be lovers and friends. Courage requires acting even in the face of fear. Refuse to allow your HIV+ diagnosis or any illness to be an albatross around your neck. While you do not have to wear a sign around your neck advertising that you have received an HIV+ diagnosis, it is still important to realize that others have legitimate fears, considering what they think they know. They are doing the best they can with what they know and with what they have been taught. Respect that. Being honest about your experience of having received an HIV+ diagnosis.

What I do is bring up the subject of having received an HIV+ diagnosis early-on, though not too early. I discuss my views and experiences with HIV and allow others to consider their own views, thoughts and feelings about my story—my story of transcendence. I use those situations as opportunities to plant seeds of awareness, the awareness that HIV is a hoax and lead them to the truth about HIV antibody testing!

Some of your potential partners will be compassionate and understanding. Others will fade out of your life, fearing becoming contaminated. Well, that is just something that you have to learn to deal with. Having them fade away is good for you. It lets you know that they are not the right person for you. Have faith and know that the right person(s) for you is out there and that and will be drawn to you at the appropriate time. Remember, however, that not everybody is meant to be in a love relationship. You might be one of those people. That is not an experience that your soul seeks to have in this lifetime, and that is okay.

Accept life as it is and always look for ways to become a better, more spiritually-focused person despite appearances in this world of illusions. Only love is real. While you might not like the answers that life sometimes provides for you, you must accept things as they are and do all you can to make them better. Who knew that better than enslaved- ancestors? They loved in spite of hatred. They endured through tribulation for the sake of future generations, for life is truly eternal.

Do not isolate, motivate! Get out there and do like I do. Take action. Speak your piece. Help others pierce the veil of illusion and emerge into the *Light of Truth,* the truth that there is no HIV and that we are not victims. We are powerful creators of our world.

As you continue on your spiritual journey, I know that you will and as I do. You will see and experience life from a new and exciting perspective. Everything and everyone in the world has meaning and purpose. We are all connected. We are all one. You will come to know yourself as a powerful creator.

> *"Knowing is not enough. We must apply. Willing is not enough. We must take action."*
>
> Bruce Lee

HIV/AIDS Speak

"All war is based on deception." Sun Tzu

I want to speak about the Language of Death that many people have allowed themselves to adopt. Words and phrases like HIV Status, HIV Virus, The Package, AIDS Virus, AIDS Infection, Viral Load, Full-Blown AIDS, T-Cell Count, Know Your Status, etc… have been aggressively marketed and have become part of the well-designed, intended and crafted language/lexicon of death that keeps the masses of people living in fear of sex and sexuality and in fear of "The Virus" that was never purified and isolated and proved to exist from the very beginning. Why? Because the entire HIV paradigm is based on the false premise that HIV was purified and isolated. It never was.

Discussions about how to keep oneself (HIV-) are taking place in various groups of well-meaning people who have not researched the other side of the crisis and come to a logical conclusion that HIV does not exist, only the HIV antibody test exists. Ironically, a few people who were diagnosed HIV+ are claiming they have taken HIV drugs as prescribed for years and that their health is better for it. These type statements and claims are simply not true. It is impossible to not have experienced the detrimental direct effects of ingesting drugs that block the synthesis of DNA at the mitochondrial level.

HIV never existed except in the minds of the masses of manipulated people who have allowed themselves to buy into a continual blitz and media campaign that propagates the existence of HIV.

What does an HIV antibody tests prove? It proves that the person who took the test reacted to the 10 proteins tested for. Whether the definition in their part of the world requires a reaction to 2 or 3 of the 10 proteins, or 6 or 7 of them as in some parts of the world, their so-called HIV antibody test results can render them HIV+. What does that really mean, to be HIV+? Honestly, it means nothing of relevance to health. It means that the fear of death will cause a drastic shift in vibrational energy within the person and manifest as physical symptoms that most people attribute to a virus that was never isolated. It means that unsuspecting people will allow themselves to ingest prescribed highly-toxic drugs, sometimes for years. It means that the areas where "colored"/more-*melanated* people live, HIV testing is encouraged and marketed more heavily, and that an HIV positive test result is more likely to happen than among other races of people.

Again, HIV antibody test results mean nothing of relevance to your health. What it means is that are railroaded into a death campaign that will allow others to continue to profit from your demise. It means that world populations diminish. It means that mind-control and manipulation through sexual fear continues to be engrained in the consciousness of the ignorant masses of people who have been led astray from the truth about HIV. It means that genocide and eugenics has effectively been launched and maintained. Millions of dollars will continue to be garnered by so called researchers, philanthropists, activist groups of all types of people who have jumped aboard a train that literally goes nowhere fast, except into their own pockets in the form of dollars. I do, however, respect and admire the continued compassion toward those who comfort and encourage people whose life has been stained and stigmatized by a so called HIV positive diagnosis.

I asked a respected nutrition scientist and acquaintance, Cal Crilly, whom I rely on to break things down in layman's terms for me regarding HIV/AIDS Speak, a few questions. I defer to Cal from time to time for clarification about all the HIV/AIDS Speak (language and lexicon of death) that seems to keep people imprisoned by the idea that HIV exists. Here is what he had to say:

"They are just doing a magic trick. T-cells, for example, have retroviruses jumping around. So do white blood cells, all baby cells and reproductive cells have even more retroviruses. Sperm and oocytes have retroviruses. You name a cell and it will have retroviruses. The placenta and babies have the highest concentration, which is why I'm a dissident.

They call them all "endogenous". The so called HIV virus gets called "exogenous". You'll see retroviral researchers say at the beginning of research articles 'the exogenous HIV virus that causes AIDS'. They may not even believe that, but it keeps funding rolling in. Then they do big blurbs on the endogenous retroviruses, but because they said 'HIV exists' almost like a clause, by saying 'HIV exists', it covers their arses if put somewhere in their article. HIV sequences are so amazing at mutating that there is not one single HIV in anyone and from organ to organ HIV 'sequences' vary. It's all rubbish and clearly a genetic part of humans and monkeys and mammals.

It's a magician holding up a hat full of retroviruses and saying, 'here I found the HIV virus and it causes AIDS'.

To be taken seriously by the mainstream, you simply stop saying 'HIV doesn't exist', because that helps them paint you as some sort of crazy, because the machines are picking up retroviruses. But if you simply ask these lunatics 'how do the HIV tests tell the difference between the 8% retroviruses in our DNA and so called 'HIV'?' then you have them stumped and they start running, simple question change. They can't answer that because the HIV antibody test does not actually pick up a HIV antibody, and the PCR viral load detects the same retroviral particles that appear in cancer, leukemia, arthritis, lupus, psoriasis, MS, Crohn's and pregnancy anyway. Sick t-cells are jumping with retroviruses in anyone who is sick. The claim that they are infected is insane.

Also, by stating HIV doesn't exist, you have then have made yourself an expert so you have to answer their bizarre claims. By asking the other question, they have to answer, so you just shoot down their claims methodically, and their massive bunker ends up burning in on itself.

That's the best way of describing what I know. Here's an example, an overview of how retroviruses are involved in development; that means babies and stem cells growing. At the start of the article they throw in the "HIV exists and is infectious" clause to keep their funding rolling, or they may even believe it, because of 30 years of University propaganda, but the rest of the article is about babies, genetics and retroviruses. "Close to half of the human genome is derived from retrotransposons replicating by the copy-and-paste mechanism used by exogenous retroviruses such as HIV. Dynamic control of endogenous retroviruses during development http://www.sciencedirect.com/.../pii/S0042682210007518."

In response to my **"Melanin Theory"** hunch, which asserted that "more-melanated" peoples of color are under attack by a genocide and eugenics campaign through HIV Antibody Testing procedures that look for signs of potential spiritual unfoldment and evolvement, which when it identifies those markers in the DNA, targets those people for destruction through fear-propaganda and prescribed highly toxic drugs that block the synthesis of DNA, Mr. Crilly responded:

"…even without a melanin theory, I say this in all sincerity and people think I'm joking but I'm not. I actually think these people are quite thick, plus they are supreme wankers, and they will bully their way to the top to get a grab of the top dog scientist thing, once you step into this virus world and believe it and have the gear, people give you importance for finding bits of viruses that have been in us since we were sludge. I

truly believe they made up HIV because they believed pygmies eating monkeys passed it through the Congo to people who went to Haiti where gays on sex tours contracted AIDS. If you look at the beginnings of this, that is exactly what they were trying to prove. So really you're dealing with red neck racists given a degree or two and some labs to go ballistic with.

If you test African people over and over and over again, then it's like bingo! That's why people who test over and over and over again often are negative at times, bingo test..."

(Hehe), I would like to use a nicer word than wankers, but it's the main one that fits. You don't see them testing white people all the time. There are genes I believe that make Africans cross-react more, but it reflects certain genes that occur in Africans, and whites with arthritis and lupus. It's really more like bingo. Gays, for instance, are said to be HIV + more only because they test them more. Plus, the main reason for an 'epidemic' in places like South Africa are because they continually test women at the maternity centres, and pregnancy is when our retroviruses become the most active.

It's back to the magic hat analogy, they test African mums over and over and their placentas are full of retroviruses anyway. They really believe the Pygmy theory and Monkey out of Africa stuff too. Sad world of scientists. They see what they want to see."

They are racists who believe they'll find HIV in Africans so they look, find a few bits that look like 'HIV', and say here is the retrovirus from the hat full of retroviruses. Keep things short or your mind will get into overdrive. They are just racists in lab coats with degrees and some fancy sounding machines."

I hope that the scientists among us learn of the secrets of melanin. Black people, unlike white people are carbon-beings, not carbon-based beings. Melanin is a superconductor that holds the key to unlocking genetic memory. It is the most primitive and universal pigment in living organisms produced in the pineal gland which controls all mental and physical body activities. It is an extremely stable molecule that is highly resistant to digestion by most acids, and melanin is one of the hardest molecules to ever be analyzed. High levels of melanin in a person allows them to heal faster, think clearer, perform greater, not to mention dawn spiritual abilities of telepathy and other abilities that I believe are lying dormant all people, at least in those who are "ensoulled", and who have more melanin, not just melanocytes. Melanin is essential for conveying energy. When sunlight hits a person with melanin, that person becomes charged like a battery with energy, not burned by the rays of the sun.

Whether others like hearing that or not, it is the science behind what I believe to be an incessant assault on people of color all over the planet, not just with HIV Antibody testing, but every other facet of systemic oppression and discrimination.

Is it not a scientific fact that ARVs block the synthesis of DNA at the mitochondrial level? Yes, science has rendered that in fact, ARVs block the synthesis of DNA at the mitochondrial level. I experienced that first-hand. That was not an apparition. It was the direct effect of ingesting prescribed, highly-toxic drugs that I was told were going to help me. Shame on my doctors for submitting me to such so-called treatment. Shame on them for killing masses of unsuspecting people for all these years.

I also advise people not to allow anybody to tamper with their blood and gain access to their DNA, or submit their children to the administration of psychotropic drugs. As a former special education teacher for students with so-called Behavior Disorders mostly Black boys who had been routed into self-contained education classes away from the larger student body, I resigned when I was required to deliver the drugs to the children on schedule. I would not be party to a system designed to harm Back boys. I fully intend to get to the bottom of these horrible atrocities, including the thousands of "missing persons", Black, melanated people of color, and the reported organ harvesting of melanated people.

Heed my advice. Never take an HIV antibody test without being informed about what it actually does. HIV antibody testing is dangerous to your physical, mental, emotional and spiritual health. I suggest that you educate yourself and others and stop allowing the world to run amok in insanity with the idea that HIV is real. I encourage those who have tested so called HIV negative to educate themselves and unpin their badge of honor. Most importantly, I support any message that encourages responsible sexual behavior inclusive of the energy of love for everybody on the planet. That responsibility lies in educating yourself to the truth about HIV.

Sigil Magic and
AIDS Iconography

"...and this is where the Magic happens."

I would like to call to your attention the construction of Sigil Magic, HIV/AIDS sigils. Symbols are sigils. Sigils are magical signs: a sign or image that is supposed to have magical power. http://www. mookychick.co.uk/health/spirituality/magical_sigils.php The AIDS ribbon iconography has always given me pause. Its color is red. Red represents the color of the root chakra where one's energies are grounded to the earth, one's family or tribe, and one's community. When root chakra energies are grounded, we are safe. People diagnosed HIV positive sometimes lose to that necessary connection. Their basic survival needs are threatened. Energy is depleted from the root chakra when they experience rejection and lack of love and support from close others.

Certainly receiving a so called HIV+ diagnosis causes root chakra energy disturbance and imbalance. I have long said that physical symptoms from purported HIV are caused by root chakra disturbances and energetic imbalance.

Think about it. The red AIDS ribbon is most certainly not shaped like the **ANKH**, which is the symbol for *eternal life*. Rather the red AIDS ribbon can be viewed as being a symbol of death. There is always meaning in symbol design. People wear them when their loved ones have died from so-called HIV/AIDS.

People wear the AIDS ribbon when raising money to show their support for the cause of helping bring an end to the HIV crisis. In my view, the "AIDS Establishment" is a money-making-murder-machine disguised as philanthropy. Supporters as well as its victims are largely unaware of the travesties being committed. The AIDS ribbon is a carefully crafted sigil that affects people on a subconscious level.

A quick comparison of the AIDS ribbon and the ANKH symbol can be easily reveal that they are opposites. I suggest to you that the AIDS ribbon is an anti-life sigil/symbol hidden in plain sight.

Flip the script. Go from death to life.

HIV Badge of Honor

"Unpin your HIV Badge of Honor." –Damian Laster

A difficult but necessary conversation must be held about people who wear their so-called HIV status like a badge of honor. So-called HIV negative (HIV-) people frequently act as if their behavior or lack of sexual behavior or so-called protected, safe-sex practices are the reason that they have tested HIV-. They think like that because they were conditioned to believe the lie of HIV. They have not thoroughly researched the crisis for themselves. As a result, serious ego issues within them have resulted, a third chakra imbalance phenomenon. These people have been so mind-controlled by this hoax that they want credit and to be well-thought of for not testing so called HIV+, as if they are somehow better than those who do test HIV+. Many of them actively and passively put-down and vilify even their friends who tested so-called HIV+.

In an effort to prop up their own ego and figure out a way to survive the genocidal attack on their life, even people diagnosed so-called HIV+ have embraced their so-called HIV diagnosis. They say things like, "I'm Poz and Proud". They have embraced an identification that is not based in truth. They are affirming an illness that they do not have, owning what is not theirs to own.

Saying that HIV exists does not make it so without scientific proof.

Both groups of mis-educated and misguided people have embraced an identification that is not based on scientific evidence. When the truth about HIV is revealed, their trained mis-educated, mis-guided view of HIV will reveal a kind of insanity that has become commonplace and replete in society. The language and lexicon of death through "HIV/AIDS SPEAK" (T-Cell Count, Viral-Load, Anti-retrovirus, HIV Test, AIDS Infection, HIV Positive, GRID, and the infamous one that rolls off the tongue of almost every human who has fallen for the HOAX, "THE VIRUS") has firmly taken root in their consciousness and dulled their minds to critical thinking and analysis. They have willingly evaded critical thinking by not researching for themselves and arriving at the conclusion that there is no HIV. The conspiracy to confuse, make ill and kill has worked like a charm for those who have created the lie of HIV and the myth of AIDS.

No, you are not better because you tested so-called HIV negative. No, it is not okay to identify with a disease that is not yours.

The intended and well-designed and crafted language/lexicon of death keeps the masses of people living in fear of sex and sexuality, and leads them like cattle to the slaughter, right into the hands of those who disdain them and who benefit and profit from their demise. Words and phrases like HIV status, full-blown AIDS, HIV virus, AIDS virus, AIDS infection, Viral load, t-cell count, know your status, testing makes us stronger, etc....have been aggressively marketed to a fearful public via mass media. Just because a lie is repeated over and over and over does not make it true.

So few people have yet to learn and accept that HIV was never isolated from the very beginning of this crisis. Toxic living and toxic lifestyles caused physical illnesses and death in the early days of the crisis. They have accepted a paradigm that is false.

The simple truth is that I and many others who came to our senses and removed ourselves from the clutches of insanity and saved ourselves by changing our consciousness and lifestyle habits. We healed our mind, healed our emotions, healed our body and healed our spirit. We healed our soul. We are free from the clutches of HIV insanity.

Discussions about how to keep oneself so-called HIV negative are taking place in various groups of well-meaning people, most of whom have not themselves received an HIV+ diagnosis, and who have not researched the other side of this crisis. They do not yet know that there is no HIV virus; only an HIV antibody test exists and purports its existence. The very people who are scaring you to death have not been directly impacted by an HIV+ diagnosis. The so-called scientists that we are supposed to trust have miserably failed us.

What is also similarly startling and ridiculous is the people who were diagnosed HIV+ who claimed that they have taken the ARV drugs and have been helped by them. They claim they are now healthy. They claim that they have taken their ARVs as prescribed drugs for many years. These statements are simply not true. ARVs are antibiotic initially and do help people show signs of healing for a few weeks, but when taken for prolonged periods of time lead to debilitating direct effects, discussed earlier. Unless what they are ingesting is placebo, it is impossible not to experience the direct effects of ingesting highly toxic drugs that block the synthesis of DNA and remain healthy with no visible signs of harm to the body. These people are lying if they are taking ARVs as prescribed.

I have talked with several people who received an HIV+ diagnosis who only took a pill or two or more from time to time, probably after worry and guilt set in after occasional sexual trysts. I used to be one of those people.

I am boldly stating that HIV never existed, except in the minds of the masses of manipulated *"sheeple"* who have allowed themselves to buy into a continual advertising blitz and media campaign that propagates the existence of a non-proved HIV virus.

What does HIV antibody testing prove? It proves that the person who took the test reacted to the proteins tested for. Whether the definition of what it means to be HIV+ in their part of the world requires a reaction to 2 or 3 of the proteins, or 4 or 5 of them, their co-called HIV antibody test results can render them accused of harboring a seemingly deadly diagnosis.

What does it mean to test HIV+?

➢ It means that the fear of death along with shame and guilt from receiving an HIV+ diagnosis will cause a drastic shift in vibrational energy within the person.

➢ It means that unsuspecting people will allow themselves to ingest prescribed highly-toxic drugs, sometimes for years.

➢ It means that the geographic locations were colored/more *melanated* people live, HIV antibody testing will be encouraged and marketed more heavily.

➢ It means that an HIV+ antibody test result will more likely happen for Black people than for any other race of people.

➢ It means that, frankly, an HIV+ or HIV- test result means anything other than to those whose continued profits soar from the administration of the test and the marketing and selling of toxic drugs.

➢ It means world populations diminish.

➢ It means that mind-control, domination and manipulation through sexual fear is further engrained into the consciousness of the ignorant masses of people who have been easily led astray from truth.

➢ It means that the genocide and eugenics campaign has effectively been launched and maintained.

➢ It means that this fiasco has been allowed for over 30 years.

➢ It means that dollars and grants are garnered by so-called researchers, philanthropists, politicians and activist groups of all types who have jumped aboard a money train that goes mostly into their own pockets.

***I implore you to never take an HIV antibody test without researching the HIV dissenting perspective. HIV antibody testing is dangerous to your mental, emotional, spiritual and physical health. Take it from me. I saved myself 18 years ago in 1998. I would be six feet under had I continued to listen to the very people I was taught to trust.

I meet people daily who have educated themselves to the other side of this crisis, the dissent perspective of HIV. They saved themselves just like I did.

I hope we continue to do all we can to stop allowing the world to run amok in insanity.

I do, however, respect and admire the continued appreciation for those who comfort and encourage people whose lives and reputations have been tarnished and whose health was diminished after receiving an HIV+ diagnosis. I have every faith that they, too, will heal***

Unpin Your HIV Badge of Honor. It is time to re-educate yourselves and apologize to those you offended. Get back to living in truth instead of continuing to live in illusion and be the loving, nonjudgmental person you were born to be.

HIV Stigma and Lack
of Social Support

"Action always beats intention."

HIV Stigma fuels the fire of the HIV HOAX

I decided that I will earn a PhD. in The Psychology of Mental Health Counseling after completing the Master of Psychology at Capella University. I intend to show the evidence for introducing the HIV Dissent perspective. Here is one way I advocate for HIV dissent in the university setting at the graduate school level. I will continue to expose the truth about HIV antibody testing. When the truth about HIV is known and accepted, HIV Stigma will ultimately be removed from the consciousness of humanity.

Introduction

This research project examined HIV Stigma (HS) and Social Support SS) for people diagnosed HIV positive (HIV+), and determined that HS and SS is a worldwide problem. HS resulted in depression, isolation, oppression, discrimination, rejection, mental health problems, career loss, substance abuse, suicidal ideation. People diagnosed HIV+ felt stigmatized and had higher levels of depression, and experienced alcohol and substance use and abuse. Fear was associated with blood transfusions and disclosure of HIV+ diagnosis. ARV drug regimens were shown to not be adhered to by people who were diagnosed HIV+. The research also showed that HS was directly correlated with low SS. In other words, higher levels of HS were associated with lowered levels of SS. HIV dissent is a worthy area for further and future research, as it will present new levels of consciousness awareness about disease manifestation and why HIV is thought to be not proved to exist and verified by science. Overall health through effective program development to address reducing and eradicating HS while increasing SS, and improving quality of life (QOL) for people diagnosed HIV+ is warranted. Additionally, alternative and holistic health care, inclusive of emotion-focused coping and informational support, can be provided

197

to educate people who receive an HIV+ diagnosis, their families, the larger community and the world, in an effort to reduce HIV stigma.

Literature Review

Earnshaw, Lang, Lippitt, Jin, Chaudoir, 2014 showed that despite efforts, societal stigma threatens the health of people diagnosed HIV+. The stress associated with lack of familial and community support was associated with purported HIV symptoms related to stress. In fact, no resources kept people diagnosed HIV+ from the harmful effects of HIV Stigma. I hope to fill the gap in research at the post graduate school doctoral level by finding out if Earnshaw et al.'s research can be refuted, and perhaps amended upon further examination of this issue, to determine what can effectively be done to diminish HIV Stigma and increase Social Support to improve the health of people diagnosed HIV+.

Farber, Lamis, Shahane, Campos, 2014 showed that HS represented a source of major stress in one mental health services program. Their cross-sectional investigation examined associations between SS and perceived HS, which resulted from blaming and distancing that people imposed on people diagnosed HIV+. The blaming dynamic was negatively correlated with stigma. However, SS mediated positive personal meaning, distancing and blaming.

People who stigmatize persons diagnosed HIV+ vary across age, culture, race, religion, socioeconomic strata, educational level and every other category with one thing in common: averse and adverse reactions from most people toward those diagnosed HIV+. A review of the literature showed that the main factors that contributed to HS was the belief that people who received an HIV+ diagnoses were personally irresponsible and promiscuous.

HIV Stigma was pervasive in religious groups as well. The church held moral and religious beliefs, which taught that guilt and punishment for immoral behavior resulted in receiving an HIV + diagnosis. These will be explored as contributors to HS. Consequently, people diagnosed HIV+ were feared, demonized and set apart from the larger community as they are viewed as potential contagions and sexual contaminators. Moreover, the physical effects on a person's appearance due to the effects of ARV therapy resulted in forced disclosure of HIV status, and the stigmatizing of people who were diagnosed HIV+.

The impact of receiving an HIV+ diagnosis is a complex issue. Themes were revealed: issues about difficulties disclosing status, medication adherence, psychological, social and emotional burdens that lead to social and relationship problems in families and intimate relationships. Participants reported having experienced abandonment from friends and family, threats of loss of employment, eviction from their homes, diminished in self-esteem, denial of professional services, loss of hope and changes in plans and loss of hope for future aspirations. The negative effects of stress on adolescents has been largely understudied, but adult studies have allowed for conceptualization of how adolescents might be affected. They too, were highly stigmatized by what is thought to be a life-threatening illness. As a result of HIV stigma, the participants reported depression and severe hopelessness that was not contaminated by physical symptoms, yet anger has been found to be a common emotional reaction that led to diseases like diabetes.

Loss of reputation, diminished self-concept and self-esteem resulted in feelings of worthlessness, job loss and loss of income, despair, depression, PTSD, and suicidal ideation that often bring clients in for counseling treatment as determined by researchers in this literature review. Ban Ki Moon, The Avert National Secretary, said that HIV stigma was the single most important barrier to public action http://www.avert.org/hiv-aids-stigma-and-discrimination.htm.

People tended to avoid seeking help when they experienced physical and emotional symptoms of diseases and illnesses when they perceive that they were are HIV-related.

Research Methodology/Data Analysis

Qualitative and Quantitative Research Methodology

Qualitative research design is one way researchers studied personal meanings, intimate relationships and in-depth holistic perspectives of people whose are shaped by their environment and the events of their lives. Researchers gained valuable insight and information through participants' descriptive renderings of life events in interviews. Qualitative analysis is not hard science. It allowed participants to freedom to use their own language to express themselves to the best of their ability (Houser, 2015). Qualitative research analysis involved organizing, categorizing and looking for patterns in the data collected. The researcher eliminated personal involvement in phenomenological Research, examined, clusters, and synthesized the data into meaningful information (Houser, 2015).

Qualitative researcher allowed flexibility to gain understanding of unusual or exceptional situations without having to utilize extensive or expensive resources. It was the responsibility of the researchers to recognize potential for bias in the collection of data to increase opportunities to generalize their results of research to the larger population. The methods chosen protected the privacy of the participants whether the approach and research design method chosen was a case study, ethnographic study, grounded theory, historical or a phenomenological approach that helped researchers understand how humans developed a way of knowing their world (Houser, 2015).

Both qualitative and quantitative research methods were used to study HS and SS Foster, Pamela, P., & Gaskins, Susan W. (2009). One empirical study was both qualitative and quantitative and utilized interviews and focus groups who described their HIV related stigma experiences. Twenty four (24) men and women over the age of 50 who were diagnosed HIV+ were audiotaped and transcribed for analysis.

Comparative data analysis obtained from stigma scales revealed 4 themes: acceptance of the disease, disclosure, stigma experiences and the need for HIV education. Internalized shame was the most significant factor but not actual stigma itself that affected people diagnosed HIV+ in that study. Intervention efforts related to programs directed at reducing shame and improving social support were implicated. The usual demographic categories were considered along with how it was perceived to have been allegedly contracted, whether from sexual contact or blood transfusion or injection drug use.

Adolescents and HIV Stigma and Social Support

The purported so-called HIV virus was said to have affected 34 million people in the world according to the United Nations Program. Women, minorities and children ages 13-21 were diagnosed HIV+ at alarmingly ever-increasing rates. These people were presumed to have been sexually active and therefore so-called "infected" in adolescence

http://www.niaid.nih.gov/topics/hivaids/Pages/Default.aspx.

Hosek (2005) studied HS and SS in adolescent HIV+ participants using quantitative methods. Current interventions are aimed at increasing anti-retroviral (ARV) medication adherence among people diagnosed HIV+. Adolescents between the ages of 16 and 24 were studied. 17 females, 25 males participated. 66% had missed a dose of medicine in the past week while 42% missed a dose yesterday. Depression and age of first marijuana use was determined by regression analyses and demonstrated that first use of marijuana, as predicted, was statistically significant in predicted higher rates of non-adherence. Interestingly, 69% of adolescents ages 16 to 24 had yet to begin the transition from concrete thinking to formal/abstract reasoning ability.

Mental Health Impact of HS and SS

Li, Li, & Lee, S. J., & Thammawijaya, P., & Jiraphongsa, C., & Rotheram-Borus (1984) uncovered a less studied dimension of worldwide HS and SS that typically accompanied the well-known ones that included oppression, discrimination, fear, and rejection, The dimension of loneliness was studied to determine how it impacted mental health. A gap was revealed. The personal stress and associated social inequality kept persons diagnosed HIV+ from seeking counseling help. A randomized controlled intervention trial for families in Thailand was performed in this quantitative research study. HS measures were adapted from scales. Composite variables from subscales of emotional/informational/affectionate support in the Medical Outcomes Study Social Support Scale yielded correlations between those variables.

112 HIV+ male and female participants ranged in age from 23 to 64 (average age 37), education and income level. As predicted and hypothesized, higher levels of depression were prevalent among people living with HIV stigma and lack of social support. Continued intervention programs that promote diminished stigma and promote increased social support were implicated.

Mental Health and Antiretroviral Drugs (ARVs) and HS/SS

The physical effects on a person's appearance due to the effects of ARV therapy resulted in forced disclosure of HIV status and the resulting stigmatization of people diagnosed HIV+. Reuda, S., & Gibson, K., & Rourke, S., & Bekele, T., & Gardner, S., & Cairney, J. (2012) showed that HS was associated with depressive symptoms. The purpose of the study was to examine (mastery) or internal psychosocial resource and control over the forces in one's life, versus (support) or the interpersonal relationships, networks and social interactions) available to people. Results indicated that a sense of mastery and personal control over one's health and life moderated the negative effects of HIV stigma and depressive symptoms, while SS did not.

825 participants were studied. Researchers controlled for potential clinical and demographic cofounders. Data was collected from structured interviews. The independent variables of age, race, gender, personal income, employment status, sexuality (straight/gay/bisexual) were tabled. The results were consistent with other cross-sectional studies that show that social support moderates depressive symptoms. The implications for mental health counseling were to consider whether a client diagnosed HIV + was at a necessary level of mastery that would allow counselors to consider appropriate treatment approaches.

In Australia, 20 gay men who were diagnosed HIV+ between the ages of 22 and 49 talked about ARV therapy in interviews. They discussed drug treatment regimens and morale concerns. Participants did not want to begin therapy in the absence of physical symptoms. They did not want to be monitored and pressured to start ARVs Gold, Ron S. (2001). Further, the physical effects a person's appearance due to the effects of ARV therapy resulted in forced disclosure of HIV status which resulted in HIV stigmatization.

Multicultural Concerns and Research Methods

Demeke (2014) showed that HIV stigma disproportionately affected African Americans. He found that native born African-American HS as determined by the Brief COPE scale, other scales, and medical outcomes showed that foreign-born Blacks were less likely than native-born Black participants in the study to disclose, cope and receive SS. They tended to avoid coping more than native-born Blacks. Native-born participants were also likely to be heterosexual, female, non-smoker, non-drinker, women living with someone, where foreign born Blacks who were stigmatized were more likely to be male/female, homosexual, homo and hetero sexual prostitutes and hustlers, drug users and people with low-income. Foreign-born African Americans were also less likely to disclose that they had been diagnosed HIV+. Demeke's results revealed implications for targeting interventions for coping and increasing social support programs which would support African Americans who are disproportionately diagnosed HIV+.

Caribbean and African American HIV+ women were also studied by Logie, C., & James, L., & Tharoa, W., & Louty, M., (2013). Their quantitative research contributed to the understanding of the association between the independent variable of race and gender discrimination. They revealed an association between HIV stigma and social support on the dependent variable, depression. They used a multi-method, community based cross-sectional survey and utilized the Brief Resilient Coping Scale and the BDI-FS. 173 women non-randomized women participated in the survey. Further, the study stated that women were greatly overrepresented in the so-called "new infections" category, and they experienced gender discrimination, barriers to treatment and mental health problems that stemmed from HS. A descriptive analysis was performed. Moderation and mediation analyses and block regression measured the associations between HS, gender and race discrimination. Moderation and mediation through SS yielded the result that resilient coping was associated with reduced depression, but did not reduce HS. It was indicated that greater micro-interventions that counsel and teach coping skills for depression and programs that challenge social stigma can promote mental health.

Researchers who created this quantitative research study hypothesized that SS can serve to protect African-Americans from stress, negativity, and discrimination resulting from HS. Correlations between 283 HIV+ African-Americans (70% men, 25% women, 4% transgender) were recruited from a cross-sectional sample. The purpose of the research was to examine the relationships between perceived HS and perceived SS. Gender, age, sexuality, income, education, annual income, living situation, depression, and alcohol use, abuse or dependence. A gap in the research revealed a need for further research on people diagnosed HIV+ who exhibited maladaptive alcohol consumption when they perceived that they had little SS. Women, on the one hand, feared stigma and lack of support from friends, family, church congregants, and health care professionals. On the other, men feared self-disclosure.

Interestingly, the researchers mentioned, however, that African-Americans had higher HS from their families than Whites who were diagnosed HIV+. As well, there were a broader range of perspectives about stigma from African-Americans than other races. Nevertheless, when support went up, perceived stigma went down. Programs that advocate and teach less ruminating can result in better mental health.

In Australia 20 gay men who were diagnosed HIV+ between the ages of 22 and 49 talked about ARV therapy in interviews. They discussed drug treatment regimens and morale concerns. Participants did not want to begin therapy in the absence of physical symptoms. They did not want to be monitored and pressured to start ARVs.

In China, HIV stigma and social support was also studied among injection drug users in China at a drug clinic. The purpose of the study was to examine relationships between mental health and their caregivers using quantitative measures. Multivariate linear regression analysis showed that the strongest predictor of poor caregiving was HS, which resulted in low levels of SS that also affected the caregivers' stress, burden and psychological health, which in turn, affected caregiving and patient care. 110% of eligible participants agreed to be assessed using the Hospital Assessment for Depression Scale (HADS). 96 patients participated. Demographic and medical covariates between patient and caregiver were statistically evaluated using a t-test for continuous variables. Demographic factors included age, sex, education, family health history, personal health history, substance abuse history, relationship status (S or M), and mental health were factored. As hypothesized, caregivers' poor mental health status affected their ability to provide care to people diagnosed HIV+ who were also injection drug Greene, M. C., & Zhang, J., & Desai, M., & Kershaw, T., 2013.

Media and Internet and HIV Stigma and Social Support

People diagnosed HIV+ turned to the media and internet to garner support for HS and SS. A qualitative study researched media practices of people diagnosed HIV+ who sought internet support as a strategy for self-representation. Themes included autobiography, expertise, self-promotion and activism for public health issues related to HIV diagnosis. One ethnographic study filled the gap by studying internet sites where people presented autobiographies, expertise and self-promotion from an HIV dissenter's perspective. It is believed that there is a connection between media activism and people who use the internet as a forum for activism. Public health problems and issues can be addressed and expressed on the internet in ways that are omitted by other media. There are gaps in the research for people diagnosed

HIV positive (+). Race and geographic location are factors (Gillett, James, 2003).

Peter, Meylakhs, & Yuri, Rykov, & Olessia, Koltsova, & Sergey, Koltsoy (2014) completed an interesting qualitative internet research study called, An AIDS-Denialist Online Community on a Russian Social Networking Service: Patterns of Interactions with Newcomers and Rhetorical Strategies of Persuasion.

"Netnography" allowed for a method of collecting data at least 2-3 times a week for 9 months by periodically downloading community discussions for qualitative analysis. The AIDS "Denialist" communities showed patterns of interactions to newcomers to the group and showed rhetorical strategies that "denialists" used for persuasion and to compel the veracity of their views. 4821 posts and comments were analyzed. Grounded theory was used for data analysis. Most people came to the discussions because their personal stories did not fit or support the prevailing HIV paradigm. Doubters were undecided in their views about HIV. "Denialists" refuted it. Orthodox views held fast to the purported science and propaganda. Reception ranged from convinced to cold or slightly hostile to extremely hostile.

Regardless of widespread public opinion and the widespread depiction of HIV/AIDS, AIDS "Denialists" suspected that something was wrong with the so-called scientific theory of HIV/AIDS and had sufficient grounds challenge the prevailing paradigm. The research suggested that health care workers change from a one-size-fits all mode of counseling, to one that addresses the unique and complex needs of people diagnosed HIV+ because of pervasive scientific uncertainty.

Implications for Future Research

Continued research can be helpful when determining problems, making and testing hypotheses, collecting and analyzing the data, and designing programs that address prevention, Intervention, and mental health programs to help address and educate people diagnosed HIV+, their families, communities and the larger world population around these issues. An effective counselor I will be able to assist my clients through the healing process and improvement of the QOL of their life having endured the trauma and stress of receiving an HIV+ diagnosis.

How will I do that? I know first-hand the importance of reducing HIV stigma in the consciousness of clients, spouses, children, families and the larger community. Increasing social support through education can be a way to do that and enhanced caregiving for HIV clients, their families and the larger community http://www.avert.org/hiv-aids-stigma-and-discrimination.htm.

Alternative Health Care for People Diagnosed HIV+

Holistic and alternative health care improved and increased SS. Emotion-focused coping and informational support increased physical and emotional health and increased life span and improved QOL. Slater, Moneyham, Vance, Raper, Mugovero, and Childs (2013) showed that social support was positively and significantly correlated with QOL, while medical comorbidities, social stigma and emotion-focused coping and social support were negatively correlated with QOL. People who died, did so because of medical conditions simultaneously occurring in the patient, not from an HIV virus. Slater et al. (2013) also showed that the life expectancy of people living with HIV improved the QOL in older homosexual men who received SS, emotional support and informational support.

Multicultural Health Care Disparities

Earnshaw, V. A., & Bogart, L. M., & Dovidio, J., & Williams D. R. (2013) showed disparities in health care for racial and ethnic peoples that resulted in racial segregation, internalized stigma and multiple stigmas that manifested as traumatic assaults, psychological injury, cultural destruction, displacement, land loss and slavery, as well as diminished life-span.

Native-American/Alaskan natives, Blacks and Latinos were found to suffer more than Whites. These scholars' peer-reviewed research supported an empowerment agenda, resilience and innovative interventions to reduced disparities and increased social support for people diagnosed HIV+.

Additional Cultural Considerations

HIV Stigma (HS) and Social Support (SS) is a worldwide problem. Research showed problems exist in The U.S., China, Africa, Canada, Thailand, Australia and other areas of the world. HS and SS affected Blacks, Latinos, Whites, Native Americans, Men, women and children of all ages, races and religions, and resulted in oppression, discrimination, and rejection. People diagnosed HIV+ felt stigmatized, had higher levels of depression, mental health concerns and experienced alcohol and substance use and abuse. Fear was associated with blood transfusions and disclosure of so-called HIV status. There were also issues with HS and SS among drug injection users. ARV drug regimens were shown to not be adhered to by people who were diagnosed HIV+. HS was directly correlated with low SS.

Caribbean, African and Black women who are diagnosed HIV Caribbean and African American HIV+ women were also studied by

Logie, C., & James, L., & Tharoa, W., & Louty, M., (2013) conducted a study to contribute to the understanding of association between the independent variable of race and gender discrimination, stigma and social support on the dependent variable, depression. This multi-method, community based cross-sectional survey utilized the Brief Resilient Coping Scale and the BDI-FS. 173 women non-randomized women participated in the survey. Further, the study stated that women were greatly overrepresented in the so-called "new infections" category, and they experience gender discrimination, barriers to treatment and mental health problems that stem from HIV stigma. A descriptive analysis was performed. Moderation and mediation analyses and block regression measured the associations between HIV stigma, gender and race discrimination. Moderation and mediation through social support yielded the result that resilient coping was associated with reduced depression, but did not reduce HIV stigma. It was indicated that greater micro-intervention that counsel and teach coping skills for depression and programs that challenge social stigma can promote mental health.

In China, HIV stigma and social support was also studied among injection drug users in China at a drug clinic. The purpose of the study was to examine relationships between mental health and their caregivers using quantitative measures. Multivariate linear regression analysis showed that the strongest predictor of poor caregiving was HS, which resulted in low levels of SS that also affected the caregivers' stress, burden and psychological health, which in turn, affected caregiving and patient care. 110% of eligible participants agreed to be assessed using the Hospital Assessment for Depression Scale (HADS). 96 patients participated. Demographic and medical covariates between patient and caregiver were statistically evaluated using a t-test for continuous variables. Demographic factors included age, sex, education, family health history, personal health history, substance abuse history, relationship status (S or M), and mental health were factored. As hypothesized, caregivers' poor mental health status affected their ability to provide care to people diagnosed HIV+ who were also injection drug Greene, M. C., & Zhang, J., & Desai, M., & Kershaw, T., 2013.

With respect to HS and SS and ARVs quantitative measures were aimed at increasing antiretroviral (ARV) medication adherence among people diagnosed HIV+. In one study of adolescents between the ages of 16 and 24, was comprised of 17 females, 25 males participated. 66% had missed a dose of medicine in the past week while 42% missed a dose yesterday. Depression and age of first marijuana use was determined by regression analyses and demonstrated that first use of marijuana, as predicted, was statistically significant in predicted higher rates of non-adherence. Interestingly, 69% of adolescents ages 16 to 24 had yet to begin the transition from concrete thinking to formal/abstract reasoning ability.

In one qualitative study, "Psychological and social difficulties of adolescents living with HIV: A qualitative analysis", researchers interviewed eight (8) 17 to 21 year old people diagnosed HIV+. The participants, described as "Key informants" included 3 males and 5 females and were paid $15. Interestingly, one male participant refused the compensation saying that speaking about these issues benefitted him. Five of the 8 participants identified themselves as African-American, 1 Latino, 1 multiracial, 1 (other) identified as Jamaican.

Flyers were handed directly to the case managers, doctors, psychologists and other researchers who already had established relationships with the participants. A convenience sample was established from a medical center/hospital located in a Midwestern city in the US. The time lapse between the date of diagnosis and this study was 2 months to 4 years. Because of their young ages, probability sampling was not possible so a convenience sample was used. Written parental consent of participants between the ages of 18 and 21 had to be obtained. The fact that HIV+ is considered to be a STD, obtaining parental consent could prove to be an explosive situation resulting in abuse, psychological distress and further stigmatization that they described as "never going away" saying people who thought you were a nice person now "just hate you". Participants also reported distancing and isolating from their peers, avoiding friendships and being exiled from their families when they revealed their HIV+ diagnosis. Others reported being afraid that they could inadvertently kill others. It was also revealed that people preferred to take vitamins daily instead of prescribed ARVs for the rest of their lives. The idea of that "freaked them out". Few adhered to medication regimens. Nausea, loss of appetite were the reasons for not adhering. One person said, "I just stopped taking it...that shit made me feel horrible...I have too much garbage on my mind to be thinking about what time to take a pill." Generalizability of this study was limited by convenience sampling, yet it was determined that continued collaborative relationships and efforts be forged to create effective prevention and intervention programs.

Ban Ki Moon, The Avert National Secretary has said that HIV stigma is the single most important barrier to public action http://www.avert.org/hiv-aids-stigma-and-discrimination.htm. People tended to avoid seeking help when they experienced physical and emotional symptoms of disease. Nevertheless, because of the fear of social disgrace and HIV Stigma, people were less likely to seek help for their illnesses even when they perceived that they were HIV-related. It is my hope that doing this research study will continue to develop improved Social Support programs that allow the mental counseling professionals to help reduce fear-based HIV Stigma, self-stigma and social stigma, while increasing Social Support and enhanced caregiving for HIV clients, their families and the larger community.

Practice and Implications of the Research

The loss of reputation, diminished self-concept and self-esteem can result in feelings of worthlessness, job loss and loss of income, despair, depression, PTSD and suicidal ideation that often bring clients in for counseling treatment. An effective counselor can assist their clients through the healing process and improvement of the QOL. How? By understanding the importance of reducing HIV stigma in the consciousness of clients, spouses, children, families and the larger community, thereby increasing Social Support http://www.avert.org/hiv-aids-stigma-and-discrimination.htm.

Holistic and alternative health care, improved and increased social support, emotion-focused coping and informational support can increase physical and emotional health, increase life span and improve QOL. Slater, Moneyham, Vance, Raper, Mugovero, and Childs, 2013 showed that social support was positively and significantly correlated with QOL, while medical comorbidities, social stigma and emotion-focused coping and social support were negatively correlated with QOL. In other words, the people who died did so because of medical conditions simultaneously occurring in the patient, not from an HIV virus. Slater et al. (2013) also showed that the life expectancy of people living with HIV has improved the QOL in older homosexual men who receive social, emotional and informational support. Alternative medical systems that involved mind-body interventions, energy therapies and other less conventional treatments experienced less side effects than they did from ARVs interventions (Konnifall and Lillisand, 2006).

HIV Dissent/Looking Ahead

The topic of HIV Dissent was not, however, the focus of the research, but looking ahead shall be the focus of future research. This research project provided the backdrop for understanding experiences and observations about ways to reduce future HIV Stigma through HIV Dissent education, which can increase Social Support that is so important to the profession of mental health counseling (MHC). At the post-graduate school level, research design and analysis can be explored from this important perspective. This missing link will fill the gap that exists because of the misunderstanding of the difference between HIV and HIV Antibody Testing. In other words, information regarding what HIV is and what HIV is not can be taught.

The Case Against HIV (Bauer, 2014) provided a comprehensive overview of the results of questioning thousands of people most of who were experts in their science fields about HIV/AIDS. The HIV/AIDS dissidents' data demonstrated conclusively that HIV is not sufficient or necessary to cause AIDS. Award-winning documentaries, videos, films, articles and books included Continuum magazine, Positively False—Birth of a Heresy, House of Numbers, etc., shed much light on the promulgated views about HIV that were thrust into the public sphere. The results of his study is study challenged everything about the prevailing paradigm of HIV as well as the alleged beneficial effects of ARV prescribed drug administration.

Results indicated:

1. There is no gold standard test for HIV.
2. HIV does not destroy the immune system. People of African ancestry tested HIV+ more than any other race of people.
3. HIV does not cause AIDS, and HIV and AIDS are not correlated in any way.
4. HIV tests have never been shown to detect HIV.
5. HIV was never isolated and purified by classical methods of virology.

6. Electron micrographs did not show a virus, but show dead cellular-debris.
7. HIV tests are not valid.
8. HIV tests detect antibodies not virus.
9. The belief that the detection of antibodies indicate earlier exposure, not infection, and in the absence of symptoms of illness would necessarily mean immunity as a result of prior infection.
10. Viral load measurements cannot be reproduced are not specific to presumed HIV and therefore is not a marker for risk of death or progression of disease.

The list goes on and on and on and on and on.….

Counselors with established professional identities as HIV dissenters can work with HIV+ clients. Having experience with HS and low SS after receiving an HIV+ diagnosis, the impact from discrimination, rejection, homophobia, alcohol and drug use and abuse, negative attitudes, maltreatment, career loss can be treated.

Inconsistencies in HIV antibody testing can be exposed. He research currently clearly shows that many clients do not adhere to prescribed ARV regimens citing their negative effects. Spirituality and alternative/holistic health care modalities can be can allow clients a choice in their treatment approaches. There is opportunity to advocate for social justice and ethical standards for people diagnosed HIV+.

Peer reviewed scholarly literature regarding HIV Dissent can be greatly improved. There is little if any available in school databases. The agenda of the journal owners can be researched to determine why that is the case. There can be study to determine what the HIV dissent perspective has been withheld from public consciousness. One example of this very phenomenon is when Bruce Charlton, professor of theoretical medicine and creator of Medical Hypotheses, a journal known for its radical and dissenting agenda, came under fire by their publisher Elsevier when they allowed the publication of an article that claimed that there was no proof that HIV causes AIDS http://www.nature.com/news/2010/100318/full/news.2010.132.html.

What some say could potentially be potentially dangerous to public health, others contend shall be **revolutionary**. This **revolution** will accompany and assist the current and evolving shift during this Age of Information, Age of Enlightenment and Age of Technology, Age of Truth.

Every research study in this project study that involved ARVs, showed that people did not adhere to prescribed drug regimens because of their negative effects. The researchers had hypothesized that reducing HS and improving SS would increase ARV adherence. It did not.

Creative Research design that addresses HIV dissent can help narrow the gaps in research by providing positive informational, educational and emotional support to people diagnosed HIV +. Given their new awareness about the HIV Dissenting perspective, people will have an opportunity to educate themselves and make health care decisions from a place of awareness, rather than relying on others to dictate how they manage their health care. They will have a choice whether to remove themselves from what some scientists and scholars say is a false paradigm. Mental Health clients can also decide for themselves whether to cease their prescribed toxic drug regimens, heal their bodies, regain their mental and emotional stability, and live longer, healthier lives. Enhanced and improved support for people diagnosed HIV+ by educating the masses starting at the individual, family and community level, and later branching out to the world community, will allow counselors to counsel HIV+ clients effectively. Exposing inconsistencies in HIV testing can lead to refusal to take the test.

The QOL for all people on the planet will improve when the HIV Dissent perspective is allowed to come to awareness of the people, and is no longer squelched by the scientific community, big media, pharmaceutical companies and misguided philanthropic organizations.

I hope to help others improve their QOL and increase the lifespan of people diagnosed HIV+ by eliminating HIV Stigma and increasing Social Support, while stimulating resilience. HIV dissent awareness can reduce HIV Stigma and consequently increase Social Support, and improve physical, emotional and mental health of all people.

Physical symptoms of disease are self-created from prolonged states of a consciousness of fear, shame and debilitating guilt (Hay, 1984, 1987, 2004). Physical symptoms of disease were not the result of a never before isolated and purified HIV virus. "Up to today there is no single scientifically really convincing evidence for the existence of HIV. Not even one such retrovirus has been isolated and purified by the methods of classical virology" (Dr. Heinz Ludwig Sanger, Emeritus Professor of Molecular Biology and Virology, Max-Plank Institute for Biochenistry, Munchen. http://www.virusmyth.com/aids/books.htm.

Astoundingly, even the HIV Antibody Test Kit says on the label itself that the test is not approved by the Food and Drug Administration (FDA) for identifying an HIV Virus http://www.omsj.org/blogs/hiv-tests-explained.

Respected HIV dissent agencies like Virus Myth http://virusmyth.org/, Alberta Reappraising AIDS literature review at http://aras.ab.ca/top10.html, Rethinking AIDS http://www.rethinkingaids.com/ The Office of Medical and Scientific Justice http://www.omsj.org/, The Perth Group http://www.theperthgroup.com/, and any organization(s) that has respectably and effectively challenged the HIV/AIDS hypothesis for over 30 years. Many medical doctors, persons with

PH.D.s and other educated scholars have published books. Authors and scientists like Dr. Henry Bauer http://www.jpands.org/vol12no4/bauer.pdf, Dr. Nancy Turner-Banks, M.D., and others. President Thabo Mbeki of South Africa, Celia Farber, Christine Johnson, Cal Crilly, Dr. David Rasnik, Dr. Peter Deusberg, Dr. Kary Mullis and others' works can be explored. Knowledge of their perspectives can reduce HS, deception and misunderstanding of the truth about HIV http://www.virusmyth.com/aids/books.htm.

Among the more popular books available on topic of HIV dissent include AIDS, Opium, Diamonds and Empire: "The Deadly Virus of International Greed", "The AIDS War", "AIDS, Inc.", "Deadly Deception", "Inventing the AIDS Virus", "Positively False", and "Impure Science", and many others http://www.virusmyth.com/aids/books.htm. The HIV/AIDS has been being questioned for over 30 years http://journal.frontiersin.org/Journal/10.3389/fpubh.2014.00154/full.

Continued contribution toward reducing HIV Stigma will be the publication of THERE IS NO HIV: The Rainbow Warrior Exposing The Truth about HIV Antibody Testing, and The Metaphysics of Self-Healing Through Chakra and Kundalini Awareness by Dr. Damian Q. Laster, Msc.D., M.Ed. I have long held that what is missing is an understanding of the spiritual component, and the knowledge of the awareness that people are responsible for creating their physical symptoms that they have associated with a never before isolated HIV virus. Their symptoms are created from ill states of consciousness, and can be self-healed by restoring energetic balance to their body through Chakra and Kundalini Awareness, Meditation, Relaxation and Spirit Guidance.

Other sources of information are also available which clearly show how HIV Stigma is a worldwide problem. Video documentaries that question HIV include "House of Numbers" http://www.youtube.

com/watch?v=BwgmzbnckII, "HIV/AIDS: Fact or Fiction" http://
www.youtube.com/watch?v=9pLUfZsKSYE, and radio interviews of
credentialed and respected doctors, nutritionists, scholars and people
directly impacted by an HIV+ diagnosis. They are available on the
subject of HIV from the scholarly perspective of HIV dissent by
Harvard Medical School graduate, Dr. Nancy-Turner Banks http://
www.youtube.com/watch?v=31QwnTt0YgM.

Conclusion

Loss of reputation, diminished self-concept and self-esteem can
result in feelings of worthlessness, job loss and loss of income, despair,
depression, PTSD, and suicidal ideation that often bring clients in
for counseling treatment. An effective counselor can assist their
clients through the healing process and improvement of the QOL.
By understanding the importance of reducing HIV stigma in the
consciousness of clients, spouses, children, families and the larger
community thereby increasing Social Support http://www.avert.org/
hiv-aids-stigma-and-discrimination.htm.

HIV Stigma (HS) and Social Support SS) is clearly a worldwide
problem which results in oppression, discrimination, isolation and
rejection, stigmatization, depression, suicidal ideation, alcohol and
substance abuse. Fear was associated with blood transfusions and
disclosure of HIV+ diagnosis. People do not adhere to ARV drug
regimens. HS was directly correlated with low SS. People of all ages,
races, cultures, mostly people of color are impacted after receiving an
HIV+ diagnosis. Low levels of social support can be increased with
education and program development.

Great opportunity exists to educate people and have them be better
able to decide for themselves what to think and feel about HIV and how

to make informed health care decisions for themselves in conjunction with health care professionals and mental health counselors.

People will be aware of and given access to information withheld from them by big media outlets, big pharmaceutical companies, doctors, pastors, HIV/AIDS philanthropic agencies and organizations and all others who currently are not vested in the truth about HIV, or the largely unknown dissenting perspective. Educating people diagnosed HIV+, their families, professionals, communities and the world about HIV will drive my social justice advocacy efforts. Further research of HIV, HIV Stigma (HS) and Social Support (SS) shall lay the groundwork for eliminating HS and the need for SS.

References

http://aras.ab.ca/top10.html. Retrieved October 24, 2014.

http://www.avert.org/hiv-aids-stigma-and-discrimination.htm Retrieved October 24, 2014.

Baeur, Henry, http://www.jpands.org/vol12no4/bauer.pdf. Retrieved October25, 2014.

http://thecaseagainsthiv.net/ Retrieved Dec.10, 2014.

http://www.counseling.org/resources/aca-code-of-ethics.pdf Retrieved November 13, 2014.

Demeke, Hanna Bewketu, 2014. Relationships between HIV-related stigma, coping, social support and health-related quality of life in people living with HIV/AIDS. *Dissertation Abstracts International: Section B: The Sciences and Engineering, 74 (11-B)(E).*

https://www.counseling.org/docs/competencies/ multcultural competencies.pdf?sfvrsn=5 Retrieved November, 13, 2014.

Earnshaw, V. A., & Lang, S. M., & Lippitt, M., & Chaudoir, S., 2014. HIV

Stigma and physical health symptoms: Do social support, adaptive coping, and/or centrality act as resilience resources? *AIDS and Behavior, April 9.*

Farber, E. W., & Lamis, D. A., & Shahane, A. A., & Campos, P. E., 2014. Personal meaning, social support, and perceived stigma in individuals receiving HIV mental health services.

Foster, Pamela, P., & Gaskins, Susan W., Older African Americans' management of HIV/AIDS stigma, 2009. *AIDS Care, 21*(10), 1306-1312.

Galvan, F. H., & Davis, E. M., & Banks, D., & Bing, E. G., HIV stigma and social support among African Americans. *AIDS Patient Care and STDs, 22*(5), 423-436.

Gillett, James, 2003. Media activism and Internet use by people with HIV/AIDS. *Sociology of Health & Illness, 25*(6), 608-624.

Gold, Ron S., 2001 I will start treatment when I think the time is right: HIV positive gay men talk about their decision not to access antiretroviral therapy. *AIDS Care, 13*(6), 693-708.

Greene, M. C., & Zhang, J., & Desai, M., & Kershaw, T., 2013. Mental health and social support among HIV positive injection drug users and their caregivers in China. *AIDS and Behavior, 17*(5), 1775-1784.

Hay, Louise, L., 1984, 1987, 2004. You Can Heal Your Life, Hay House, Inc.

http://www.youtube.com/watch?v=9pLUfZsKSYE HIV AIDS: Fact or Fiction, Retrieved October 25, 2014.

www.henryhbauer.homestead.-com Retrieved Dec 11, 2014.

http://www.youtube.com/watch?v=BwgmzbnckII House of Numbers, Retrieved October 25, 2014.

Houser, Rick, 2015. Counseling and educational research: Evaluation and application, 3rd edition. SAGE Publications, Inc.

http://journal.frontiersin.org/Journal/10.3389/fpubh.2014.00154/full Retrieved October 25, 2014.

Kahn, T. R., & Desmond, M., & Rao, D., & Marz, G.E., & Guthrie, B. L., & Bosire, R., & Choi, R., Y.,& Kiarie, J.N., & Farquhar, C., 2013. Delayed initiation of antiretroviral therapy among HIV-discordant couples in Kenya. *AIDS Care, 25*(3), 608-624.

Konefal, J., & Lillisand, J., 2006. Complementary and Holistic Medicine. *Psychiatric aspects of HIV/AIDS*, 365-377. *Journal of Clinical Psychology in Medical Settings, 21*(2), 173-182.

Konefal, J., & Lillisand, J., 2006. Complementary and Holistic Medicine. *Psychiatric aspects of HIV/AIDS*, 365-377. *Journal of Clinical Psychology in Medical Settings, 21*(2), 173-182.

Li, Li, & Lee, S. J., & Thammawijaya, P., & Jiraphongsa, C., & Rotheram-Borus, 1984.Stigma, social support, and depression among people living with HIV in Thailand. *AIDS Care, 21*(8), 1007-1013.

Logie, C., & James, L., & Tharoa, W., & Louty, M., 2013. Associations between HIV related stigma, racial discrimination, gender discrimination, and depression among HIV positive, Caribbean, and Black women in Ontario, Canada. *AIDS Patient Care and STDs, 27*(2), 114-122.

http://www.nature.com/news/2010/100318/full/news.2010.132.html. Retrieved October 25, 2014.

http://www.niaid.nih.gov/topics/hivaids/Pages/Default.aspx Retrieved October 2, 2014.

http://www.omsj.org/. Office of Medical and Scientific Justice Retrieved October 23, 2014.

http://www.omsj.org/blogs/hiv-tests-explained Office of Medical and Scientific Justice Retrieved October 26, 2014.

Peter, Meylakhs, & Yuri, Rykov, & Olessia, Koltsova, & Sergey, Koltsoy (2014) completed an interesting qualitative internet research study called, An AIDS-Denialist Online Community on a Russian Social National Research University Higher School of Economics, Laboratory for Internet Studies, St. Petersburg, Russian Federation

http://www.jmir.org/2014/11/e261 Retrieved December 9, 2014.

http://www.rethinkingaids.com/ Retrieved October 23, 2014.

http://rethinkingaids.com/quotes/test-false-positive.html Retrieved October 25, 2014.

Reuda, S, & Gibson, K., & Rourke, S. B., & Bekele, T., & Gardner, S., & Cairney, J., 2012. Mastery moderates the negative effect of stigma on depressive symptoms in people living with HIV. *AIDS and Behavior, 16(3)*. 690-699.

Slater, L. Z. & Moneyham, L., & Raper, J. L., & Mugavero, M. J., & Childs, G., 2013.

Support, stigma, health, coping, and quality of life in older gay men with HIV. *JANAC: Journal of the Association of Nurses in AIDS Care, 24*(1), 38-49.

http://www.virusmyth.com/aids/books.htm Retrieved October 24, 2014.

http://www.youtube.com/watch?v=31QwnTt0YgM Retrieved October 25, 2014.

Wohl, A. R., & Galvan, F. H., & Carlos, J., & Myers, H. F., & Garland, W., & Witt, D., & Cadden, J., Operskalski, E., & Jordan, W., & George, S., 2013. A comparison of MSM stigma, HIV stigma and depression in HIV-positive Latino and African American men who have sex with men (MSM). *AIDS and Behavior, 17*(4), 1454-1464.

Consultation and
Social Justice Advocacy

"Take action. Do not be silent."

In the speech "Challenge to The Nation's Social Scientists" in September of 1969, Rev. Dr. Martin Luther King, Jr. spoke at a convention sponsored by the American Psychological Association (APA). Paraphrasing, Dr. King eloquently advised that, "destructive maladjustment" should be eradicated, and that to avoid schizophrenia and neuroses, everyone must seek to live a "well-adjusted" life. He articulated that we should never adjust to physical violence, unfair economic conditions, religious bigotry, militarism, segregation and discrimination (Roysircar, 2009). Dr. King was a "social justice extraordinaire." He, others, and I believe that counselors have a responsibility to not only heal self, but also to heal society.

I believe we can infer that Dr. King was speaking about any unfair discrimination or institutionalized oppression that existed in the world. When I become a mental health counselor, aside from my general responsibilities, I will work to provide dissenting views and information regarding HIV, HIV antibody testing, and treatments to the public. I feel it is my moral duty, in light of my personal experiences, to provide information about holistic and alternative therapies for improving overall health, perhaps without the need for and administration of toxic prescription drugs for children, adolescents and adults. I will continue to stress the importance of proper nutrition as a most important factor for healing any and all disease. I am obliged to provide the best possible care to my clients.

I accept the responsibility to be an advocate for all of my clients. I know that my HIV dissenting views to the idea that "HIV is the cause of AIDS" shall be presented to all who are able to receive that knowledge. I will help others learn to make informed decisions about their own health.

Some people who experienced *Kundalini awakening* experienced spiritual emergency and/or spiritual crisis, and were incorrectly diagnosed with Schizophrenia (Collie, 1996). They can receive information about the characteristics of spiritual awakening phenomenon, along with opportunities to receive drug-free treatments that can include alternative and holistic therapies (Shore, 1997).

Newman and Newman (2012) defined an advocate as a person who pleads another's case. Advocacy and social justice topics have a rich tradition and can be integrated from a multicultural perspective (Steel, J., 2008). (Glossuf, Durham, 2010) said that there is a need for both diversity in orientation to social justice, as well as a need for strategies that can to help teach others to become social justice advocates. Constantine, Hage, Kindaichi, & Bryant, 2007; Crethar, Torres Rivera, & Nash, 2008; Hays, Dean, & Chang, 2007; Roysircar, 2009 said that we can be self-reflective of oppression in our own life to be effective social justice advocates.

There can be no social justice where truth and honesty is not present. In addition, as an advocate for and consultant to those who are diagnosed with schizophrenia, I will use approved assessment instruments and other methods to help determine if such a diagnosis is correct and determine if the patient or client is experiencing spiritual emergency/spiritual crisis. I will provide opportunities for them to consider non-invasive methods of treatment. People in spiritual crisis can be encouraged to participate in the planning of their treatment.

The National Institute for Mental Health (NIMH), in response to concerns from clinical researchers and advocacy groups for patients, sponsored a workshop that addressed the controversial impact of drug-free periods, during the course of both HIV and Schizophrenia (Shore, 1997). They addressed concerns about those patients who, because of their health, were not able to make informed decisions for themselves regarding the administration of prescribed drugs into their body. Many people diagnosed with Schizophrenia are mis-diagnosed (El Collie, 1996). These people are not schizophrenic, but are in spiritual crisis.

As a result of my dynamic Kundalini Awakening, I can help others through the lens of my own experiences. Lives will be saved by advising, where appropriate, that people be educated about the dangers of toxic prescription drugs for HIV/AIDS as well as for Schizophrenia.

People going through a spiritual crisis are really experiencing an "ego death." Unsuccessful and old ways of being are dying, and sometimes leave the person feeling despair and hopelessness. The resultant inner chaos is sometimes mis-diagnosed as schizophrenia or bipolar disorder.

My own personal experiences left me feeling, for a time, that God had forsaken me. But after intense research to understand what was happening in my body and in my life, I was able to distinguish for myself that my experiences were not psychotic in nature, or indicative of mental illness, but were related to the powerful consciousness-transforming energetic force known as Kundalini. A spiritual transformation was taking place.

Christina Groff, founder of the Spiritual Crisis Network, and author of The Search for Wholeness, along with her husband, the renowned Dr. Stanislov Groff, author of books including *The Stormy Search for Self, Beyond Death, and Spiritual Emergency*, taught the phenomenon known as Kundalini Awakening, and offered breath-work exercises, meditation and relaxation, as well as a variety of other strategies to soothe the patients' anxieties and symptoms. They, too, supported that if a person chose to, they would be able to use those strategies without the use of prescription drugs and/or psychiatry (Mishlove, 1999). http://www.intuition.org/txt/cgrof2.htm).

In an article called "Misdiagnosis" published by one Kundalini Support Group called *Shared Transformation, El Collie (1996)*, the group's founder, informed that a wide variety of somatic disorders are experienced during spiritual crisis. These disorders might include epilepsy, low back problems, inflammatory disease, heart and panic attacks, irritable bowel syndrome and bipolar disorder and depression. Yet, they are not the result of psychiatric disorders.

In my role as a teacher, healer and shaman and social justice advocate, I plan to continue to share with others what I learned from my traumatic experience of living through the HIV/AIDS debacle and crisis; knowledge about HIV antibody testing, and dissenting views to HIV being the cause of AIDS. People I encounter who suffer from receiving an HIV positive diagnosis will be given the opportunity to make more informed decisions about treating their health issues. I believe that as people are educated to their spiritual nature, they will begin to understand that they are spiritual beings having a physical experience, and that they can heal the underlying causes of their diseases by healing the consciousness that created them. Awareness and knowledge of the human body chakra system can provide alternative and holistic healing methods and treatments, perhaps to go along with other healing modalities, of which there are many.

Sadly, not one, but two of my acquaintances, in separate incidents, literally leaped from a bridge to end their own life, as a result of receiving an HIV + diagnosis. One of them ended his own life. The other one was subsequently hospitalized in a mental health institution. Many acquaintances of mine abused alcohol and/or legal/illegal drugs. Brakoulis (2006) confirmed that some schizophrenics became suicidal, or abused drugs, or inflicted self-harm. In truth, are not all self-destructive behaviors indicative of inflicting self-harm? I think they are.

It is difficult if not impossible to make informed decisions about one's health when there is a propagation of unfounded fears, and the distribution of misinformation designed to manipulate mass consciousness about any topic. Well-meaning philanthropists and innocent others forward misinformation when they blindly follow the television media and religious zealots, without questioning things for themselves. Unless and until people resist mind-control techniques and strategies, they will allow themselves to be blindly led by those who might not have their best interests in mind and certainly not at heart; those who seek to profit from others' misfortunes, or who might have hidden agendas. I can serve as a consultant to and an advocate for such people.

Consider the following fictitious hypothetical scenario: Bobby, a 24 year old gay, white male, is urged by HIV antibody testing advocates to take an HIV antibody test. He is told that it is best to "know your status." Test results came back HIV+. Surprised and disappointed, Bobby fears that he will die. Bobby is then counseled to see a doctor. The doctor urges Bobby to take further tests to determine his T-cell count and viral load. He begins taking prescribed AZT drugs, even though he is not sick. Bobby's mother and father were divorced after his high school graduation. He tries to communicate with his clinically depressed mother that he tested positive for HIV. Mother becomes infuriated and tells everybody that she is ashamed of him and ostracizes him from the family. Bobby's mother tells her other son and daughter he has AIDS, not that he is HIV positive, but that he has AIDS. Both of them are embarrassed and angry so they, too, ostracize him from the family. He begins to drink alcohol more frequently than he usually did, misses work repeatedly, and gets fired from his job. He later loses his apartment. Friends won't help him. No one wants to be around Bobby, because he has the "gay plague" and they fear for their own life. Out of desperation Bobby becomes a hustler selling his body and so-called protected sex to make money. That trauma causes him to become a crystal meth addict. He gets caught stealing from the grocery store and goes to jail. He is later released from jail and goes back to the same lifestyle. Two weeks later, a former sexual partner is told by a mutual friend that a friend of a friend of a friend said that he heard that Bobby was HIV positive. That guy immediately goes to take an HIV antibody test and receives a positive diagnosis, accuses Bobby of infecting him with the AIDS virus, and files charges at the police station. Represented by a court appointed public defender, Bobby receives a 25 year prison sentence for attempted murder. One night while in his cell, Bobby's feelings of guilt and shame cause him to attempt suicide. Prison official refer Bobby for mental health counseling.

What would I do as a counselor to advocate for Bobby? I would consider contacting Dr. Nancy Turner-Banks, M.D., a well-known Harvard Medical School graduate and physician, and the author of "Aids, Opium, Diamonds and Empire: The Deadly Virus of International Greed," who, among many other professional responsibilities is part team of HIV experts who testify in court to and defend people who find themselves in similar situations with the legal system. I would advise Bobby to retain an attorney and contact Clark Baker, founder of The Office of Medical and Scientific Justice (OMSJ) http://www.omsj. org/issues/ustd. To date OMSJ has won 53 cases in which people were accused, charged, or jailed for so-called sexual misconduct. Among those cases, a military soldier was acquitted of four HIV-related charges against him.

Next, I would then begin to counsel Bobby, and begin his road to recovery from PTSD, alcohol and drug abuse, and place him on suicide watch. Over time, I would gage his recovery carefully and begin to introduce alternative views about HIV by guiding him to books, articles, internet websites etc. and encouraging him to have faith that he can still lead a well-adjusted life, despite all that he has endured.

Odonnell, et al. (1999) proposed that more client-focused services to community-based clients with schizophrenia improved outcomes in client functioning and satisfaction with services. Advocating and providing consultative services to the people can address both institutional (educational, medical, mental health, governmental, societal) barriers that may be present by implementing Supportive Family Training (SFT), education and a framework for cost effective teaching about major mood disorders, problem solving and communication skills and coping and management skills (Le Gacy, Schulman, 1998). People like me can continue to provide free classes to the public and expose the AIDS Hoax. Self-healing classes can also be taught to help raise awareness in communities all across the country, and in fact the world. Counselors who consult and advocate for social justice can help people "regain their sanity and their health in a world gone mad." (Turner-Banks, 2010), and help people live lives of joy in love of self and service to others.

My Spirituality and Worldview

> *"Spirituality must be lived. All the books in the world will*
> *not help us if we do not live what we have learned."*
>
> —*Author Unknown*

Spirituality is the focus of my life. It has fast become the center of my focus as a person. It is not a religious phenomenon, but rather a personal statement of the thoughts, words and actions I choose which determine whether I will create joining or separation in my life. Consciousness, in my view is all there really is. I will continue to focus on helping others find the part of themselves and help them find and learn that every experience, in particular the seeming pitfalls, present opportunities to grow in self-awareness. As Cashwell et al. (2007) reminded us in *The Only Way Out is Through: The Peril of Spiritual Bypass*, we must not allow spirituality to allow us to avoid psychological contact with our unfinished business. We must heal ourselves physically, emotionally, and mentally, in our endeavor to be whole and well.

It is important that I am culturally competent and accept worldviews other than my own (Sue and Sue, 2013). Adopting a nonjudgmental manner of being in the world can aid me in gaining practical knowledge about the experiences of daily living, cultural background, fears, aspirations, and hopes and dreams of myself and others. I will engage in actions that create conditions that allow the best conditions for optimal development for the diverse people in our multicultural world (Sue and Sue, 2013).

We can become sensitive to the needs of other people. When we are aware of our own biases and values, are comfortable around other people, knowledgeable about oppression and skilled in working with culturally diverse groups, we can demonstrate that we are possessed of the ability to recognize institutional barriers that exist in sociopolitical systems and devise strategies to communicate effectively, intervene appropriately and help people heal (Sue and Sue, 2013). Kottler (2010) reminded us to move through our disappointments, failures and imperfections and continually revitalize ourselves, yet to not forget that we shall learn from our clients more about ourselves.

My interests shall remain in all things metaphysical and my pursuits will continue to study philosophical, historical and contemporary issues that impact people on the fringes of society, like I have often felt of myself. Fortunately for me, earlier in my 30s, I became suspicious of the education I had received. I actually cried when I realized that I knew almost nothing of what being educated really meant. Up to that point, I had received "training" and not an education. My discontent launched me on a search for truth and charted my course toward becoming truly educated. I educated myself and now know myself beyond the confines of Western education and thinking. As well, I am told that I am an Indigo Adult, Starseed and Galactic Citizen who incarnated on Earth to experience duality consciousness and merge opposites at the heart chakra and ascend to unity consciousness and bring Light to the World. I now more readily recognize when others are attempting to brainwash me, manipulate my awareness, distort truth and enslave me and others. I speak my truth as an example for others speak theirs.

My worldview and cultural heritage allow me to fully understand current socio-politico-economic issues faced by Black Americans and other minority groups, in particular sexual minorities, as well as a current healthy understanding of White culture. Nancy Boyd-Franklin (1990), drawing on her experiences as a teacher, supervisor and practitioner for black families addressed topics of skin color, kinship ties, strengths and limitations, religion and spirituality and the implications for making clinical judgments of normal and abnormal Black family interactions. She, like I, will empower myself to constructively engage family members to explore the dynamics of family secrets.

My own current spiritual focus is on forgiveness of self and others, continued resilience, goal-setting and the display of increased compassion and love for all people. I will not allow one's race, gender, sexual orientation, class or status to interfere with my professional, unbiased approaches to helping people heal by helping them identify their spiritual needs, find support in their communities, and develop their unique strengths and talents.

Self-Healing is the Remedy

Our purpose on this earth is to observe, to learn, to grow, and to love (Aboriginal Proverb).

As I mentioned in chapter 13, HIV Stigma and Lack of Social Support, I will embark on journey to obtaining a Ph.D. in The Psychology of Mental Health Counseling. I intend to show the evidence for introducing the HIV Dissent perspective into the university setting. I will continue to expose the truth about HIV antibody testing worldwide, as I do now. When the truth is known, HIV Stigma will ultimately be removed from the consciousness of humanity.

The awareness that your body is able to heal itself has been intentionally withheld. When I prove to you that there is no HIV, your consciousness of humanity will be liberated. You must take action to free yourself from illusion, addiction, anger, isolation, self-hatred and hatred of others. You can recover your losses by becoming compassionate toward yourself. Let go of Mama's god and get to know the (g)od inside you that is you. Accept your divine nature, your divine self. Accept your spiritual ankh-estors and the messages they are sending to you.

Walk away from negativity and conflict. You do not have to attend every argument that you are invited to. You can ascend to higher levels of consciousness awareness. Decide to follow the call of your soul. Awaken and expand your consciousness.

Commit to continue to find out the truth about HIV antibody testing. We are in the Age of Information and you will easily access HIV dissenting perspectives. Immediately cease allowing yourself to be bamboozled. You are not alone in this awakening. We are everywhere. Join us in awakening the rest of humanity.

Be strong. Be intelligently militant. There is no need to be arrogant or weak. Strength is the substance of who you really are.

Turn off your tell-lie-vision. Think critically about everything. Flowing with the shift in consciousness awareness that I have shared in this book with you can initially seem daunting, but is far better than being stuck in suffering.

Practice and live by the principles of the chakras. Awaken your Kundalini. Have confidence to be who you really are. Accept your sexuality. Let no one convince you that you are not deserving of love. Pray. Meditate. Breathe. Dwell in the upper room of your consciousness. Be your higher self.

Forgive yourself and others continually. Forgiveness leads to love. It is the most powerful thing you can do for yourself. Educate yourself and others. Be a demonstration of resilience. Eliminate HIV Stigma. Remember that fear kills and love heals. Smile often and make others smile. Be a friend. Heal family and community ties. Embrace those who have been diagnosed HIV+. Help them re-educate themselves. Commit to help stop genocide and eugenics. You will not be punished for speaking the truth.

Truth

No one is coming to save you. You must save yourself. Illness does not belong to you. You are pure energy and you are the healer of your own life.

You are not a victim. You too can *understand, inner-stand and over-stand* yourself as a powerful creator, a master of your *"in-vironment"*. You too can know yourself as a divine being of great worth.

Henceforth, commit to observe synchronous events that reveal to you that you drew the deceptive HIV experience into your life that you might learn of your god-self, your higher self.

Why let devils conquer when you know yourself divine?

Be who you are. Love yourself. Be well. Claim perfect health.

Metaphysician, Heal Thyself, Radiate and

Spiral Love Out Into the World.

Rainbow Warrior, there is peace in the valley. There is peace in your soul. Can you feel it?

You too can become a **RAINBOW WARRIOR**.

When you accept the truth that **THERE IS NO HIV** and live your *(g)od* self, your divinity will be a reality in your world.

I am the gardener. I have planted the seeds. It is now up to you to water the garden of your own awareness.

I am the truth. I'm The Living Proof. There Is No HIV!

*You too can be a Rainbow Warrior. You have been exposed to the truth about HIV antibody testing. You have learned the **Metaphysics of Self-Healing Through Chakra and Kundalini Awareness**.*

You are a Rainbow Warrior.

Balance dark and light.

Stand for what is right.

One Love. Choose life.

Hetep,

Damian Laster aka Kbr AmnRkhty

The Conscious Doctor/Rainbow Warrior

P.S. Take seven deep breaths. Practice The Principles of The Chakras. Awaken your Kundalini, and call me in 18 years. ☺.

Please visit my website www.consciousdr.com and utilize your Rainbow Warrior Companion.

Bibliography

http://www.abibitumikasa.com/forums/oppression-afrikans-technologically-scientifically-mathematically/40683-400-years-systemic-eugenics-race-based-genocide.html.

Afrika, L. (2000). The nutritional destruction of the Black Race, Brooklyn, New York: A& B Publishers Group.

Al-Bayati, M. (1999). Get all the facts: HIV does not cause AIDS. California: Toxi-Health International.

Alberta Reappraising AIDS Society, David R. Crowe, President. Retrieved from www.aras.ab.ca.

Arewa, C. S. (1998). Opening to spirit: Contacting the healing power of the chakras & honouring African spirituality. African World Books.

Ashby, S. M., Dr. (2003). The serpent power. Ashby Muata.

Ashby, S. M., Dr., (2005). Asarian Theology: The mystery of resurrection and immortality. African Religion Vol. 4. Cruzian Mystic Books.

Avalon, A. (Sir John Woodroffe) (1974). The serpent power: The secrets of the Tantric and Shakti Yoga. Dover Publications Inc.

Baca-Garcia, E., et al (2008). Patterns of mental health service utilization in a general hospital and outpatient mental health facilities. *European Archives of Psychiatry and Clinical Neuroscience, Vol 258*(2), 117-123.

Banks, N. T. M.D. (2010). Aids, opium, diamonds and empire: the deadly virus of international greed. *iUniverse*, Bloomington IN 46403.

Brakoulias, V. et al. (2006). Patients with deliberate self-harm seen by a consultation-liaison service. *Australasian Psychiatry*, 14(2), 192-197.

Caplan, G., et al (1994). Mental health consultation: historical background and current status. *Consulting Psychology Journal: Practice and Research, 46*(4), 2.

Cashwell, C. S., & Bentley, P. B., & Yarborough, J. P., 2007. The only way out is through: The perils of Spiritual Bypass. *Counseling & Values, 51*(2), 139-148.

Collie, E. (2012). *Osler's Web: Inside the labyrinth of the chronic-fatigue syndrome epidemic, by Hillary Johnson*. Crown Publishers, Inc., 1996. ISBN: 0-51770353-X Retrieved October 3, 2012 from http://reason.com/ blog/2012/06/12/hiv-revisionism-in-fort-bragg-acquittal

http://www.avert.org/hiv-aids-stigma-and-discrimination.htm Retrieved October 24, 2014.

Barrett, S., M.D., (2012) A close look at Robert W. Bradford and his committee for freedom of http://www.quackwatch. org/04ConsumerEducation/Nonrecorg/cfcm.html

http://biologyofkundalini.com/article.php?story= KundaliniPracticeSkillsList&mode=print.

Cady, H. E. (1995). The complete works of Emilie Cady, 1ˢᵗ edition: Lessons in truth, How I used truth, God a present help, Unity School of Christianity: Unity Books Publishers.

Carr, Ear;lene & Shurlene (1997). From the motherland to the mothership, Crystal City Publications.

Chuse, Patricia. Jepson. (1998). The godself. Patricia Jepsen Chuse Publisher.

Clear Light. http://www.clearlight.net/www.consciousdr.com Dr. Damian Laster's website.

Crilly, Cal, internet interview January 2015.

Danrich, K. (1997). Attaining the state of Christ: Lord Metatron, Lord Averil (Sai Baba) November 15, 1997. Accessed at http://www.oocities.org/yukselisorg/files/christ.html

Dale, C. (2009). The Subtle body: An encyclopedia of your energetic anatomy. Sounds True Inc.

Dale C. (2011). Kundalini: Divine energy, divine life. Llewellyn Worldwide Ltd.

Demeke, Hanna Bewketu, 2014. Relationships between HIV-related stigma, coping, social support and health-related quality of life in people living with HIV/AIDS. *Dissertation Abstracts International: Section B: The Sciences and Engineering, 74 (11-B)(E).*

http://dherbs.com/articles/aids-hiv-207.html no longer available. Can now be found November, 25, 2014 at http://www.starseeds.net/group/glbtstarseeds/forum/topics/h-i-v-aids-debunked

http://www.druidry.org/obod/lore/animal/raven.html.

Dyer, Dr. W. (1999). Manifest your destiny, becoming aware of your higher self. Harper Collins.

http://www.elcollie.com/html/Issue9a.html.

Earnshaw, V. A., & Lang, S. M., & Lippitt, M., & Chaudoir, S., 2014. HIV Stigma and physical health symptoms: Do social support, adaptive coping, and/or centrality act as resilience resources? *AIDS and Behavior, April 9.*

Eichler, A. (2012, August 9; Updated 2013, May 8). Pharmaceutical companies spent 19 times more on self-promotion than basic research: report. *The Huffington Post.* Retrieved from http://www.huffingtonpost.com/2012/08/09/pharmaceutical-companies-marketing_n_1760380.html?view=screen.

http://www.energy-healing-info.com/root-chakra.html. Retrieved September 26, 2014.

Essene, V. & Nidle, S. (1990). You are becoming a galactic human. S.E.E. Publishing Company.

Errico, R. (1994). Let there be light: The seven keys. Georgia: Noohra Foundation.

Ford, D. (1998). The dark side of the light chasers: Reclaiming your power, creativity, brilliance, and dreams. New York: The Berkley Publishing Group.

Foster, Pamela, P., & Gaskins, Susan W., Older African Americans' management of HIV/AIDS stigma, 2009. *AIDS Care, 21*(10), 1306-1312.

France, D. (2000). The HIV disbelievers. *Newsweek Magazine*. Retrieved from http://davidfrance.com/article.asp?ID=12.

Freeman, J. A. PhD & Griffin D. B. (2003). Return to glory: The powerful stirring of the Black race. Treasure House, Destiny Image Publishers, Inc.

Galvan, F. H., & Davis, E. M., & Banks, D., & Bing, E. G., HIV stigma and social support among African Americans. *AIDS Patient Care and STDs, 22*(5), 423-436.

Gillett, James, 2003. Media activism and Internet use by people with HIV/AIDS. *Sociology of Health & Illness, 25*(6), 608-624.

Glosoff, H. L. and Durham, J. C. (2010). Using supervision to prepare social justice counseling advocates. *Counselor Education and Supervision, 50*(2), 116-129.

Gold, Ron S., 2001 I will start treatment when I think the time is right: HIV positive gay men talk about their decision not to access antiretroviral therapy. *AIDS Care, 13*(6), 693-708.

Goldberg, B. (1999). Astral voyages, mastering the art of soul travel. Woodbury, MN: Llewellyn Publications.

Harrison, G. (1994). In the lap of the Buddha. Boston: Shambala.

Hay, L. L. (1984). Heal your body. Hay House, Inc.

Hay, L. L. (2004). You can heal your life. Hay House Inc.

Helpforhiv.com

Hoff, B. H. (1993) "Gays as guardians of the gates: An interview with Malidoma Somé," *MenWeb*. Retrieved from http://www.menweb. org/somegay.htm.

Horakhty, K. (2001). The rainbow warrior: Healing HIV through chakra awareness, Createspace (self-published by Odom Entertainment)

Japolsky, G. and Cirincione, D. V. (1995). Change your mind, change your life, concepts in attitudinal healing. New York: Bantam Books.

Joyce, E. "Understanding and getting familiar with the CHAKRAS – your seven energy centers - and Opening the Spiritual Chakras – 8th to 12th," *Visions of Reality*. Retrieved from http://new-visions. com/chakras/.

Kahn, T. R., & Desmond, M., & Rao, D., & Marz, G.E., & Guthrie, B. L., & Bosire, R., & Choi, R., Y., & Kiarie, J.N., & Farquhar, C., 2013. Delayed initiation of antiretroviral therapy among HIV-discordant couples in Kenya. *AIDS Care, 25*(3), 608-624.

Khalsa, Gurmukh. Kaur., Newberg, Andrew., Radha, Sivananda., Wilber, Ken., Selby, John, Kundalini Rising: Exploring The Energy Of Awakening, Sounds True Inc., 2009.

Kinslow, Frank J., The Secret of Instant Healing, Triad Publishing Group, 2008.

Konefal, J., & Lillisand, J., 2006. Complementary and Holistic Medicine. *Psychiatric aspects of HIV/AIDS*, 365-377.

Kottler, On being a therapist, 2010. Jossey-Bass, A Wiley Imprint.

Journal of Clinical Psychology in Medical Settings, 21(2), 173-182.

http://www.kundalinisupportnetwork.com/shaktipat.html.

Le Gacy, S. (2010). Working through the heart: a transpersonal approach to family support and education. *Psychiatric Rehabilitation Journal, 22*(2), 133-141.

Legion of Light (1988). Chakra awareness guide: Understanding and activating the body's seven main energy centers. Legion of Light Products.

Li, Li, & S. J., & Thamawijaya, P. & Jiraphongsa, C., & Rotheram-Borus, 1984. Stigma, social support, and depression among people living with HIV in Thailand. Aids Care, 21(8), 1007-1013.

Stigma, social support, and depression among people living with HIV in Thailand.

AIDS Care, 21(8), 1007-1013.

Logie, C., & James, L., & Tharoa, W., & Louty, M., 2013. Associations between HIV related stigma, racial discrimination, gender discrimination, and depression among IV positive, Caribbean, and Black women in Ontario, Canada. *AIDS Patient Care and STDs,* 27(2), 114-122.

Maat RA (2007) http://www.starseeds.net/group/glbtstarseeds/forum/topics/h-i-v-aids-debunked?commentId=2312030%3AComment%3A2242752&groupId=2312030%3AGroup%3A156795

Maggiore, C. (2007) If It's Not HIV, What Can Cause AIDS? *What If Everything You Thought You Knew About AIDS Was Wrong?* (p 51) New York: American Foundation for Aids.

Masachusettes News Staff (Nov, 1999). "Ritalin: Violence Against Boys." *Vaccination News.* Retrieved from http://www.vaccinationnews.org/ DailyNews/September2002/RitalinViolence30.htm.

Mierzwicki, A. "A blissful interview with Dan Winter." *New Dawn Magazine.* Retrieved from http://www.bibliotecapleyades.net/ ciencia/ciencia_danwinter13.htm.

Mishlove, J., Ph.D. (). Addiction, attachment, and spiritual crisis with Christina Grof, The Intuition Network Thinking Allowed Television Underwriter, presents the following transcript from the series Thinking Allowed, Conversations on the Leading Edge of Knowledge and Discovery with Dr. Jeffrey Mishlove. Retrieved October 2, 2012 from http://www.intuition.org/txt/cgrof2.htm.

Moe, J. L. (2010). Are consultation and social justice similar? Exploring the perceptions of professional counselors and counseling students. *Journal for Social Action and Counseling and Psychology*, Volume 2(2), 106.

Munich, R. L., (2003). Review of the environment of schizophrenia: innovations in practice, policy and communications. *Bulletin of the Menninger Clinic, 67*(4), 375-376.

Myss, Carolyn, M. (1996). The anatomy of the spirit. New York: Harmony Books/ Three Rivers Press.

Nancy Boyd-Franklin Black Families in Therapy: Understanding the African American Experience, Guilford Press.

Newman B.M. & Newman, P.R. (2012). Development through life: A psychosocial approach. (11 ed.). Wadsworth Cengage Learning.

Narby, J. (1999). The cosmic serpent: DNA and the origin of knowledge. Jeremy P Tarcher/Putnam.

http://www.nichd.nih.gov/health/topics/hiv/conditioninfo/Pages/how-many.aspx Retrieved September 16, 2014.

http://www.omsj.org/issues/ustd. Fort Bragg Acquittal OMSJ Case.

Operskalski, E., & Jordan, W., & George, S., 2013. A comparison of MSM stigma, HIV stigma and depression in HIV-positive Latino and African American men who have sex with men (MSM). *AIDS and Behavior, 17*(4), 1454-1464.

https://www.youtube.com/watch?v=QpjFN-PWxuk   Retrieved September 27, 2014.

Pierce, P. (2009). Frequency: The power of personal vibration. Atria Books.

RA, Djhuty Maat (2007) http://www.starseeds.net/group/glbtstarseeds/forum/topics/h-i-v-aids-debunked?commentId=2312030%3AComment%3A2242752&groupId=2312030%3AGroup%3A156795

Redfield, J. (1995). The Celestine prophecy and the tenth insight. New York: Warner Books.

Rist, K. J. M. D. (December 17, 1993). "HIV Infection: An Uncommon Wave of Dementia," *AIDS Treatment News*, Issue 189.

Roman, S. (1986). Personal power through awareness, Book II of the earth life series. New York: H. J. Kramer Inc., Publishers.

Roysircar, G. (2009). A study of client-focused case management and consumer advocacy: community and consumer service project. Journal of Counseling & Development, 87(3), 288-294.

Ryerson, K. and Harolde, S. (1989). Spirit communication and the soul's path. New York: Bantam Books.

Saraydarian, T. (1990). Other worlds. T.S.G. Publishing Foundation.

Shore, D. & Hsiao, J. K. (1997). Medication-free intervals and schizophrenia research: editors' introduction. *Schizophrenia Bulletin, 23(*1), 1.

Sivananda, S. Swami (1998). Mind: Its mysteries and control, The Divine Life Society.

Steele, J. M. (2008). Preparing counselors to advocate for social justice: a liberation model. *Counselor Education and Supervision, 48*(2), 74-85.

Swordtongue.com (2009). "All physical phenomena are attributes of God!" Retrieved from http://www.swordtongue.com/Godmater.html.

Teish, Luisah, 1985. Chant for self-esteem, Jumbalaya, The natural woman's book of personal charms and practical rituals http://www.reocities.com/jywanza1/Luisahteish.html Last retrieved September, 14, 2014.

The holy bible, New International Version, Grand Rapids, Michigan: Zondervan Ible Publishers, c 1973, 1978, 1984, International Bible Society.

http://www.transperception.com/chakra-diagnosis-healing.htm. Retrieved October 25, 2014.

Turner-Banks, M.D., N. (2010). AIDS, Opium, Diamonds, and Empire: The Deadly Virus of International Greed. iUniverse, Inc..

Valle'em, M. (2009). The great shift: Co-creating a new world for 2012 and beyond. Weiser Books.

http://www.virusmyth.com/aids/HIV/cjtestfp.htm

Virusmyth: A Rethinking AIDS Website. February, 2013. Accessed at http://www.virusmyth.net/aids/.

http://www.virusmyth.org.

Walsch, N. D. (1996, Conversations with god: An uncommon dialogue, Book 1. New York: Hampton Roads Publishers.

Walsch, N. D. (1997). Conversations with god: An uncommon dialogue, Book 2 New York: Hampton Roads Publishers.

Walsch, N. D. (1998). Conversations with god: An uncommon dialogue, Book 3, New York: Hampton Roads Publishers.

Walsch, N. D. (2002). Friendship with god: An uncommon dialogue. New York: Hampton Roads Publishers).

https://www.youtube.com/watch?v=7BHRV-RMNvs#t=247 Warriors of The Rainbow, Retrieved November 24, 2014.

Whitaker, S. ND, & Fleming, J., CN, MH (2005). Medisin: The causes & solutions to disease, malnutrition and the medical sins that are killing the world. Divine Protection Publications.

Weor, S. A. (2009) Kundalini yoga: The mysteries of the fire, unlock the divine spiritual power within you. Glorian Publishing.

Weor, S. A. (2010). Practical astrology: Self transformation through self-knowledge, Kabbalah, tarot, and consciousness. Glorian Publishers.

Wohl, A. R., & Galvan, F. H., & Carlos, J., & Myers, H. F., & Garland, W., & Witt, D., & Cadden, J.,

Zukov, G. (1989). The seat of the soul. New York: Simon Schuster.

Appendix A
HIV Dissent & Other Resources

Human *Immunodeficiency* **Virus** **(HIV)/Acquired Immunodeficiency Syndrome (AIDS) Dissent Resources**

Be sure to view the Rainbow Warrior Companion at www.consciousdr.com

HIV Antibody Tests Are Unreliable: *tell them you do not want the test, if you choose to do so.* You do not have to allow anybody to influence your health decisions. Arm yourself with knowledge and information. Here are the factors known to cause positive results on an HIV antibody test:

1. STREET DRUGS

2. VACCINATIONS

3. NATURALLY-OCCURRING ANTIBODIES IN BLACK PEOPLE

4. STICKY BLOOD

5. FLU OR COLD

Factors 2 - 5 are taken from http://www.virusmyth.com/aids/HIV/cjtestfp.htm (Christine Johnson)

In addition to the references listed in the Bibliography, check out the following valuable resources below. However, Be aware. The internet is a transient place. Websites move, are abandoned, lose funding, or are simply removed for one reason or another. If you find that to be the case, you can still do your own keyword search to find the truth. Nothing will stop the truth about HIV antibody testing from being revealed.

HIV/AIDS Dissent Organizations, Links and Resources

1. http://www.virusmyth.org/
2. http://aliveandwell.org/
3. http://aras.ab.ca/

HIV Dissent Videos

BEWARE: Links are sometimes removed to keep truth from being exposed. If you find that to be the case, you can still do your own keyword search and still find the truth. Nothing will stop the truth from being revealed.

1. Deconstructing the AIDS Myth http://www.youtube.com/watch?v=FRCyk0zdBxw
2. HIV AIDS Fact or Fiction: http://www.youtube.com/watch?v=0qSdvnpCfcU
3. House of Numbers: http://www.youtube.com/watch?v=BwgmzbnckII
4. AIDS is a hoax! Biologist Christl Meyer explodes the HIV/AIDS conspiracy

http://www.youtube.com/watch?v=SaA6zLUPfvk&feature= player_embedded

5. 'HIV test a crime, AIDS 'cure' killed a whole generation' https://www.youtube.com/watch?v=buoGGsch5mM Disease and States of Consciousness Featuring Dr Jewel Pookrum, M.D. http://www.youtube.com/watch?v=5AQrr2u64-c

6. EUGENICS
   If you can't handle hearing it from me, hear it from the medical doctors
   Harvard Medical School Graduate Dr. Nancy Turner Banks, M.D., author of "Aids, Opium, Diamonds and Empire : The Deadly Virus of International Greed https://www.youtube.com/watch?v=aTg7ZbtVoxM
   The Science of Panic (with subtext)
   http://vimeo.com/23068217

7. The Greatest Medical Fraud in History - The Pain, Profit and Politics https://www.youtube.com/watch?v=vT3b_0doyRk

8. Positively False: The Birth of A Heresy http://positively falsemovie.com/

Authors/Books/Interviews (Master Teachers)

1. Virus Myth Bookshelf http://virusmyth.org/aids/books.htm

2. Dr. Nancy Turner-Banks, M.D. "Aids, Opium, Diamonds and Empire: The Deadly Virus of international Greed"
   Recently removed interviews with The French Connection. Others can be found on YouTube

http://current.com/1ah3b4c

http://current.com/1q4hl4c

https://www.youtube.com/watch?v=-3wwGpO9-sU

BEWARE: LINKS ARE SOMETIMES REMOVED TO KEEP THE TRUTH FROM BEING EXPOSED. If you find that to be the case, you can still do your own keyword search and still find the truth. Nothing will stop the truth from being revealed.

Harvard Medical School Graduate Dr. Nancy Turner- Banks M.D.

Dr. Banks on So-Called HIV/AIDS. "STOP TAKING THE TEST"

1. Part 1 http://www.youtube.com/embed/4YG2b9ZzX8M
2. Part 2 https://www.youtube.com/watch?v=ekyE4S2UHLg
3. Dr. Scott Whitaker "Medisin" http://www.amazon.com/Medisin-Solutions-Disease-Malnutrition-Medical/dp/0972035222/ref=sr_1_1?s=books&ie=UTF8&qid=1329315003&sr=1-1
4. Dr. Llaila Afrika "Nutricide" http://www.amazon.com/Nutricide-Nutritional-Destruction-Black-Race/dp/1886433305/ref=sr_1_1?s=books&ie=UTF8&qid=1329314964&sr=1-
5. Keidi Awadu, The World's Leading Interviewer of HIV Dissidents http://livinginblack.ning.com/profiles/blogs/hiv-and-aids-debunked?xg_source=activity
6. Ryan Shelby Dodson : "Rethinking HIV: HIV is a Fraud", author of "Science Behind The Scam" http://www.youtube.com/watch?v=t7l1qjuaID8&feature=youtu.be
7. Dr. Jewel Pookrum M.D. Disease and States of Consciousness http://www.youtube.com/watch?v=2jvm9zgkT2Y
8. Dr. Phil Valentine on HIV/AIDS http://www.youtube.com/watch?v=SX0iOS1Ffks
9. Why HIV was Never Discovered. https://www.youtube.com/watch?v=1Ga01hvqOow

10. Positively False http://www.youtube.com/watch?v= ZAlKASzqd7I

11. (don't lie to me about HIV) Handgrenade ~ Nina Hagen https://www.youtube.com/watch?v=jwjVRL7fEyc

Books and Videos

12. VirusMyth Bookshelf http://virusmyth.org/aids/books.htm http://www.vaccinesaredangerous.com/

13. Stephen Davis, "Wrongful Death" https://www.youtube.com/watch?v=vOTnwH_wIyU

14. Djhuty Maat Ra, "HIIV/AIDS Debunked" article http://www.starseeds.net/group/glbtstarseeds/forum/topics/h-i-v-aids-debunked?commentId=2312030%3AComment%3A2242752&groupId=2312030%3AGroup%3A156795

15. Gary Null and John Rappoport expose criminals and AIDS myth https://www.youtube.com/watch?v=37AEZLZ44h0

16. MAAFA 21 [A documentary on eugenics and genocide] https://www.youtube.com/watch?v=0eWxCRReTV4

17. Christine Johnson: "Can You Really Trust the AIDS Test"? http://www.virusmyth.com/aids/hiv/chjtests1.htm

18. http://www.ourcivilisation.com/aids/hivexist/index.htm *An interview with Dr Eleni Papadopulos-Eleopulos* By Christine Johnson from *Continuum* Autumn 1997

19. Stefan Lanka Interview Why HIV has never been isolated Part 1 of 2 https://www.youtube.com/watch?v=bp2ccDup4y0&feature=gp-n-y&google_comment_id=z12qwbmh4wrpt1vta22ahttpkzmnunyq404

20. Fake A I D S H I V Diagnosis For Black People pt1 http://www.youtube.com/watch?v=2boojoJ1RnQ

21. Was HIV man made to control populations in Africa ?

HERE'S THE REALITY http://rethinkingaids.com/. The AIDS industry and media want you to believe that there are only a handful of scientists who doubt the hiv?AIDS theoryquotes/rethinkers.php

Decriminalize HIV

Because Integrity Is Worth Defending

1. OMSJ (Office of Medical and Scientific Justice) www.omsj.org
2. OMSJ Innocence Group http://www.omsj.org/innocence-group
3. OMSJ acquittals http://reason.com/blog/2012/06/12/hiv-revisionism-in-fort-bragg-acquittal www.livingwithouthivdrugs.com
4. OMSJ, HIV Drugs and The Diseases They Cause http://www.omsj.org/drugs/matrix.htm
5. www.livingwithouthivdrugs.com

Rainbow Warriors Truth About HIV Group (FaceBook)

Founder, Damian Laster

https://www.facebook.com/groups/RainbowWarriorTruthAboutHIV/

Personal Works By Damian Laster

1. **"The Rainbow Warrior: Healing H-I-V Through Chakra Awareness"**

http://www.amazon.com/s/ref=nb_sb_noss?url=search-alias%3Daps&field-keywords=The+raibow+warrior+hwealing+hiv+through+vhakras+awareness

1. **"Let HIV Set You Free"**
   http://aras.ab.ca/articles/popular/200607-Laster.html
2. **Metaphysician Heal Thyself**
   http://lightgrid.ning.com/group/7chakras12chakrasandthehigherchakraskundalinienerg/forum/topics/metaphysician-heal-thyself-a-master-s-thesis-in-metaphysical
3. **From HIV to Kundalini: Awakening the Divine Feminine Within**
   http://lightgrid.ning.com/group/7chakras12chakrasandthehigherchakraskundalinienerg/forum/topics/from-h-i-v-to-kundalini-awakening-the-divine-feminine-within-a

Use your Rainbow Warrior Companion at <u>www.consciousdr.com</u>.

***Warriors of The Rainbow* at <u>*https://www.youtube.com/watch?v=7BHRV-RMNvs#t=247*</u>**

Appendix B
Recommended Reading for the
Body, Mind, and Spirit

Acts of Faith. Iyanla Vanzant.

Adventures Beyond the Body. William Buhlman.

The African Origin of Civilization: Myth or Reality, Cheikh Ante Diop.

African Religion Vol. 4 Asarian Theology: The Mysteries of Resurrection and Immortality. Dr. Muata Ashby.

Ageless Body Timeless Mind. Deepok Chopra.

The Ancient & Shining Ones: World Myth, Magic & Religion. D. J. Conway.

The Art of Redemption. Stuart Wilde.

The Art of Spiritual Dreaming. Harold Klemp.

An Ascent to Joy. Carol Ochs.

The Astral Body. William A. E. Powell.

A Visitation of Spirits: A Novel, Randall Keenan.

A Whole New Mind: Why Right-Brainers Will Rule The Future. Daniel H. Pink.

Beyond Orion's Gates: Your Part in the War Behind All Wars. Mark A. Finley.

Bible Legacy of the Black Race, The Prophecy Fulfilled. Joyce Andrews.

Black Butterfly: An Invitation to Radical Aliveness. Richard Moss.

Black Genesis: The prehistoric Origins of Ancient Egypt. Robert Bauval & Thomas Brophy, Ph.D.

Brotherman: The Odyssey of Black Men in America, Anthology, Herb Boyd and Robert Allen.

Building The Lighted Temple: The Spiritual B-Ark: Metaphysical Keys to the Tree of Liofe & Oracle Keys to Dis-spelling Illusion. Dr. Teri Nelson/Nteri Renenet Elson.

Christianity vs Islam. The Honorable Elijah Muhammad.

The Complete Ascension Manual: How to Achieve Ascension in This Lifetime, Joshua David Stone.

Complete Works of H. Emilie Cady: Lesson in Truth, How I Used Truth, God A present Help, Emilie Cady.

Dark Matter: A Century of Speculative Fiction From The African Diaspora. Edited By Sheree R. Thomas.

Dictionary of Psychology. J.P. Chaplin, Ph.D.

Decent of The Dove. Channeled by Ann Valentin and Virginia Essene.

Divine Encounters, Zecharia Sitchin.

Divine Spirituality: Revealed Information About The Real You. Osiris Akkebala.

Eckankar: Ancient Wisdom for Today, How past lives, dreams, and Soul Travel help you find God

Egypian Heiroglyphics: How to Read and Write Them. Ste'phane Rossini.

Egyptian Yoga: The Philosophy of Enlightenment, Volume 1, Second Edition. Muata Ashby, Edited by Karen Clarke-Ashby.

Energy Anatomy. Carolyn Myss.

Finding Your Voice. Larraine R. Matusak.

Foundations of Practical Magic. Isreal Regardie.

God at the Speed of Light: The Melding of Science and Spirituality. T. Lee Bauman, M.D.

Going Home: Jesus and Buddha As Brothers. Thich Nhat Hanh.

The Great Sift: Co-Creating a New World for 2012 and Beyond. Val'ee, Ed.

The Healng Brain: How Your Mind Can Heal our Body. Emrika Padus.

Historical Deception: The Untold Story of Ancient Egypt, Moustafa Gadalla.

The History and Philosophy of the Metaphysical Movement in America. J. Stillson Judah.

How A Man Overcomes Disappointment And Burnout. David B. Hawkins, Ross A. Tunnell, III.

How You Feel Is Up To You. Mskay, Dinkmeyer.

Huna. Enid Hoffman.

Inner Perspectives: A guidebook for the Spiritual Journey. Elizabeth Clare Prophet.

In the Lap of The Buddha. Gavin Harrison.

Instant Manifestation.: The Real Secret to Attracting What You Want Right Now. Joe Vitale.

Is Jesus God? Dr. Malachi York.

Is Life A Random Walk? Harold Klemp.

The Isis Papers: The Keys to the Colors. Dr. Frances Cress Welsing.

Journey Home: A True Story of Time and Interdimensional Travel. Tonika Rinar.

Journey to The Boundless. Deepok Chopra.

Killing Rage: Ending Racism, bell hooks.

Life, Death & Consciousness: Experiences Near And After Death, Flilppo Liverziani.

Living Enlightenment: A call for evolution beyond ego. Andrew Cohen.

Losing The Race: Self-Sabotage in Black America. John WcWhorter.

Love is in The Earth Laying-On-Of-Stones: The Journey Continues. Melody.

Malcolm X on Afro-American History. Malcolm X.

The Maroon Within Us. Asa G. Hilliard.

Maximum Achievement: Strategies and Skills That Will Unlock our Hidden Powers to Succeed. Brian Tracy.

Melanin: A Key to Freedom. Richard King, M.D.

Metu Neter, Vol. 1, The Great Oracle of Tehuti and the Egyptian System of Spiritual Cultivation. RA UN NEFER AMEN.

Mindfullness: The Path to the Deathless: The Meditation Teaching of Venerable Ajahn Sumedho.

New Teachings for an Awakening Humanity. The Christ.

Of Water and The Spirit: Ritual, Magic, and Initiation of an African Shaman, Malidoma Patrice Some.

Opening to Channel. Sanaya Roman and Duane Packer.

Personal Power Through Awareness. Sanaya Roman.

Raja Yoga. Swami Vivekananda.

Receiving The Cosmic Christ: The Experience of Global Community, Shahan Jon.

Rhythms of Recovery: Trauma, Nature, And The Body. Leslie E. Korn.

Teaching to Transgress: Education as the Practice of Freedom. bell hooks.

The Bull of Ombos: Seth & Egyptian Magick II. Mogg Morgan.

The People Could Fly: American Black Folktales told by Virginia Hamilton, Illustrated by Leo and Diane Dillon.

The Power of Your Subconscious Mind. Dr. Joseph Murphy, D.R.S., Ph.D., D.D., L.L.D, Revised by Ian McMahan, PH.D.

The Secret of Instant Healing. Frank J. Kinslow.

The Secret Teachings of All The Ages. Manly P. Hall.

The Seekers Glossary of Buddhism. Edited by the Van Hien Study Group.

The Seer: The Prophetic Power of Visions, Dreams, and Open Heavens. Jim W. Goll.

The Seven Spiritual Laws of Success. Deepok Chopra.

The Sirius Mystery. Robert Temple.

Soul Retrieval: Mending the fragmented Self. Sandra Ingerman.

The Sphinx Mystery: The Forgotten Origins of the Sanctuary of Anubis, Robert Temple with Olivia Temple.

Spirit Healing. Mary Dean Atwood.

Spiritual Power, Spiritual Practice. Carolyn Myss.

Spirit Walker: Messages From The Future. Hank Wesselman.

Supernatural Assault in Ancient Egypt: Seth, Renpet & Moon Magick. Mogg Mogan.

Tankhem: Seth & Egyptian Magick. Mogg Morgan.

The Tiger's Eye. Paul Twitchell.

They Came Before Columbus, The African Presence in Ancient America. Ivan Van Sertima.

Three Levels of Power and How to Use Them. Carolyn Myss.

The Power of Now. Eckhart Tolle.

The Story of AIDS in Black America: Secret Epidemic, Jacob Levenson.

Touched By Angels. Ellen Elia Freeman.

Traveling The Interstate of Consciousness: A Driver's Instruction Manual, Using Hemisync to Access States of Non-Ordinary Reality, Patricia Levy.

The Urantia Book. Urantia Foundation.

Visions for Black Men. Na'im Akbar.

Walking On Water: Black American Lives At The Turn Of The Twenty-First Century. Randall Kenan.

The Way of The Shaman. Michael Harner.

Why People Don't Heal And How They Can. Carolyn Myss, Ph.D.

Wisdom of The Mystic Masters. Joseph J. Weed.

You Are Becoming a Galactic Human. Virginia Essene and Sheldon Nidle.

About the Author

D
r. Damian Laster, Msc.D., M.Ed., the Conscious Doctor, is System's Buster and member of the Renegade Family of Light. He is an avid HIV dissenter and social justice advocate. Dr. Laster's educational background after high school includes a Bachelor of Arts (BA) in Psychology from Birmingham-Southern College in 1986, a Master of Special Education (M.Ed.) degree in Behavior Disorders from Georgia State University in 1998 and a Doctor of Metaphysical Science degree from the University of Metaphysics at Sedona in 2011. He is currently earning a Master of Psychology in Mental Health Counseling at CACREP accredited Capella University. He exposes truth about HIV antibody testing in the university setting at the graduate school level.

Dr. Laster is also a Certified Teacher. He was an Educational Therapist, a Special Education Teacher for students with Behavioral Disorders, and a Pre-K Lead Teacher.

His scholarly writings include The Rainbow Warrior: Healing HIV through Chakra Awareness, Let HIV Set You Free, The Metaphysics of Self-Healing, and From HIV to Kundalini: Awakening the Divine Feminine Within.

Dr. Laster's community outreach efforts include work with The Office of Medical and Scientific Justice (OMSJ). He is also a member of the Rethinking AIDS Group and is the creator and founder of Rainbow Warriors Truth About HIV Group on Facebook. Dr. Laster teaches free classes at local libraries and shares HIV dissent resources at local park events.

Also know by his spiritual name Kbr AmnRkhty, which translates to mean "I AM AWARE THAT THE SPIRIT OF THE HIDDEN GOD LIVES IN ME AS THE CHRIST POTENTIAL". Dr. Laster has a keen interest in Ancient African spirituality. He is spiritual adept, teacher, healer, urban shaman, metaphysician and presenter of The Metaphysics of Self-Healing: Restoring Balance and Health through Chakra/Kundalini Awareness PowerPoint Presentation.

Dr. Laster is available for altering systems of consciousness within the freewill universe. He is dynamic and speaks for groups both large and small. Dr. Laster delivers a powerful presentation about the HIV hoax, and exposes inconsistencies in HIV antibody testing called The HIV/AIDS Trap.

Feel free to contact Damian Laster by email at dqlaster@yahoo.com. Please visit the Rainbow Warrior website www.consciousdr.com.

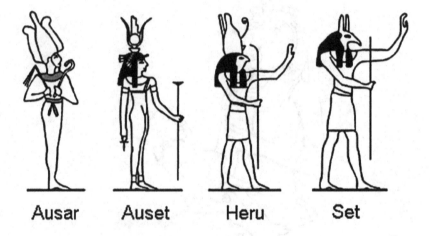

Ausar   Auset   Heru   Set